Student Resource Manual

prepared by

Jeanne Elmhorst
Albuquerque Technical-Vocational Institute

to accompany

UNDERSTANDING HUMAN COMMUNICATION

Seventh Edition

Ronald B. Adler
Santa Barbara City College

George Rodman
Brooklyn College
City University of New York

Harcourt College Publishers
Fort Worth Philadelphia San Diego New York Orlando Austin San Antonio
Toronto Montreal London Sydney Tokyo

Cover credit: Private Collection/Diana Ong/SuperStock.

ISBN: 0-15-507309-5

Address for Domestic Orders
Harcourt, Inc., 6277 Sea Harbor Drive, Orlando, FL 32887-6777
800-782-4479

Address for International Orders
International Customer Service
Harcourt, Inc., 6277 Sea Harbor Drive, Orlando, FL 32887-6777
407-345-3800
(fax) 407-345-4060
(e-mail) hbintl@harcourtbrace.com

Address for Editorial Correspondence
Harcourt College Publishers, 301 Commerce Street, Suite 3700, Fort Worth, TX 76102

Web Site Address
http://www.harcourtcollege.com

Printed in the United States of America

9 0 1 2 3 4 5 6 7 8 202 9 8 7 6 5 4 3 2 1

Harcourt College Publishers

TABLE OF CONTENTS

CHAPTER 1 HUMAN COMMUNICATION: WHAT AND WHY

CHAPTER 2 PERCEPTION, THE SELF AND COMMUNICATION

CHAPTER 3 LANGUAGE

CHAPTER 9 SOLVING PROBLEMS IN GROUPS

CHAPTER 10 CHOOSING AND DEVELOPING A TOPIC

CHAPTER 11 ORGANIZATION AND SUPPORT

'HAPTER 12 PRESENTING YOUR MESSAGE

HAPTER 13 INFORMATIVE SPEAKING

HAPTER 14 PERSUASIVE SPEAKING

Chapter 1
Human Communication: What and Why

FTER STUDYING THIS CHAPTER, YOU WILL BETTER UNDERSTAND:

1. The working definition and characteristics of communication as described in Understanding Human Communication.
2. The types of communication discussed in this book.
3. The needs satisfied by communication.
4. The characteristics of linear and transactional communication models.
5. The characteristics of communication competence and of competent communicators.
6. Common misconceptions about communication.

FTER STUDYING THIS CHAPTER, YOU WILL BE BETTER ABLE TO:

1. Define communication and give specific examples of the various types of communication and needs satisfied by communicating.
2. Discuss how the characteristics of communication apply to a specific transaction.
3. Use the criteria in this chapter to identify the degree to which behavior in a specific situation is competent, and suggest ways of increasing the competence level.
4. Identify misconceptions about communication and suggest a more accurate understanding for each.

HAPTER 1 SKELETON OUTLINE

his outline can be a helpful study tool to assist you in seeing the order and sequence of the chapter and e relationship of ideas. Use it to take notes as you read and/or to add concepts presented in lecture.

I. **COMMUNICATION IS THE PROCESS OF HUMANS RESPONDING TO SYMBOLIC BEHAVIOR.**
   - A. Communication is human.
   - B. Communication is a process.
     1. Continuous
     2. Ongoing
     3. Transactional
     4. Involves personal history contributing to your interpretation
   - C. Communication is symbolic.
     1. Symbols represent something.
     2. Symbols are arbitrarily chosen and agreed upon.

I. **TYPES OF COMMUNICATION**
   - A. Intrapersonal communication
   - B. Dyadic/interpersonal communication
   - C. Small group communication
   - D. Public communication
   - E. Mass communication

III. COMMUNICATION FUNCTIONS TO SATISFY NEEDS.

- **A.** Physical health
- **B.** Identity needs
- **C.** Social needs
- **D.** Practical needs

IV. MODELS OF COMMUNICATION

- **A.** Linear model
  - **1.** One-way activity
  - **2.** Sender, message, channel, receiver, and noise (external/physical, physiological, and psychological) environments.
- **B.** Transactional model
  - **1.** Simultaneous sending and receiving (feedback)
  - **2.** Fluid, not static
  - **3.** Relational, not individual

V. COMMUNICATION COMPETENCE

- **A.** Communication competence
  - **1.** No one, ideal way
  - **2.** Situational
  - **3.** Relational
  - **4.** Can be learned
- **B.** Competent communicators have
  - **1.** a wide range of behaviors rather than just a few.
  - **2.** the ability to choose the most appropriate behavior.
  - **3.** skill at performing behaviors.
  - **4.** empathy/perspective taking.
  - **5.** cognitive complexity.
  - **6.** self-monitoring.

VI. CORRECTING COMMON MISCONCEPTIONS

- **A.** Communication doesn't require complete understanding.
- **B.** Communication is not always a good thing.
- **C.** No single person or event causes another's reaction.
- **D.** Communication will not solve all problems.
- **E.** More communication is not always better.
- **F.** Meanings are in people, not in words.
- **G.** Communication is not simple; it is complex.

CHAPTER 1 KEY TERMS

This list of key terms corresponds to those in boldface in your text. Use these lines to write the definition and/or an example of the word on the line next to it.

channel ________________________________

____

communication ________________________________

____

mmunication competence ______________________________

____

coding ______________________________

____

adic communication ______________________________

____

coding ______________________________

____

vironment ______________________________

____

ternal noise ______________________________

____

edback ______________________________

____

entity needs ______________________________

____

teractive communication model ______________________________

____

trapersonal communication ______________________________

____

terpersonal communication ______________________________

____

ıear communication model ______________________________

____

ass communication ______________________________

____

essage ______________________________

____

noise ______________________________

____

physical needs ______________________________

____

physiological noise ______________________________

____

practical needs ______________________________

____

psychological noise ______________________________

____

public communication ______________________________

____

receiver ______________________________

____

sender ______________________________

____

small group communication ______________________________

____

social needs ______________________________

____

transactional communication model ______________________________

____

NAME ____________________

HAPTER 1. ACTIVITY 1: COMMUNICATION MODELS AND METAPHORS

URPOSES:

1. To think creatively about the transactional process of communication.
2. To construct a metaphor model to better understand communication.

NSTRUCTIONS:

1. Read the example below. Then construct and explain your own metaphor of communication, taking into account the transactional nature and elements of the communication process.

xample

raw or explain your metaphor model: Communication is like the human body.

xplanation: The body has many systems: circulatory system, gastrointestinal system, skeletal system, ervous, cardiovascular, etc. Communication has verbal and nonverbal communication, intentional and nintentional. Like the human body, you can break it down and study certain parts, but what counts is nat all are happening at once. A doctor who can't understand all the systems functioning together is not ood at diagnosing or healing. A communicator who can't analyze the parts (verbal/nonverbal, ontent/relational, intentional/unintentional) and also look at all the parts together is probably not ompetent either. If I'm injured, I expect a physician to be able to know which part to pay attention to, ut also see the relationship of all systems. I may have a broken bone, but be losing blood, too. The octor needs to prioritize and pay attention. Likewise, the competent communicator needs to see what lements of the transactional process might be causing a problem, and give attention there, while not eglecting other aspects.

here does the metaphor break down? The metaphor isn't entirely accurate because the human body is hysical; communication is relational, intangible. Communication may end in a different way than a hysical body comes to an end.

OUR TURN:

working with others, brainstorm about metaphors for communication. Choose a metaphor to explain a depth. Try to use as many principles and elements of communication as you can in explaining your etaphor and where it breaks down.

Here are ideas to start, but use your imagination: communication is like a football game, traffic atterns, the solar system, a gambling machine, the ecosystem.

raw or describe your metaphor model:

Explanation: ______________________________

____

____

____

____

____

____

____

____

____

____

Where does the metaphor break down? ______________________________

____

____

____

____

____

____

____

____

____

NAME ____________________

CHAPTER 1. ACTIVITY 2: MEETING NEEDS THROUGH COMMUNICATION

PURPOSES:

1. To classify communication behaviors with regard to what needs are met.
2. To identify ways in which behaviors meet certain communication needs.

INSTRUCTIONS:

Using newspapers or your own examples, indicate how people meet different needs through communication. One example is provided.

TYPE OF NEED MET	BEHAVIOR	HOW DID COMMUNICATION MEET THIS NEED?
Physical (health)		
Identity		
Social		
pleasure		
affection		
inclusion	Asking a co-worker if I could go with her to an after-work gathering	I'm new, so I want to feel part of this group of people at work. Going with them to a social event may help me feel like part of the group.
escape		
relaxation		
control		
Practical		

Complete the following:

Much of my communication is to meet ____________________ needs. I think this is because

____

____

Not much of my communication is for the purpose of meeting ____________________ needs.

I had most difficulty thinking of an example of how communication meets ____________________

____________________ needs.

Much of my behavior meets more than one need at once, for example, ____________________

____

____

I spend the most time meeting ____________________ needs because ____________________

____

____

I spend the least time meeting ____________________ needs because ____________________

____

____

I would like to learn to spend more time meeting ____________________ needs by (doing) __________

____

____

NAME ____________________

HAPTER 1. ACTIVITY 3: PRINCIPLES OF COMMUNICATION

URPOSE:

1. To identify and apply principles of communication.

ART 1

STRUCTIONS:

1. Using your own life and examples from current news media, give an example of each of the following:

   Communication does not require complete understanding. ____________________

   Communication is not always a good thing. ____________________

   No single person or event causes another's reaction. ____________________

   Communication will not solve all problems. ____________________

   More communication is not always better. ____________________

   Meanings are in people, not words. ____________________

   Communication is not simple. ____________________

ART 2

STRUCTIONS:

1. For each principle listed below, think of other short examples (scenes from books or films, poetry, song lyrics) that illustrate these principles.

   Meanings rest in people, not words. ____________________

   Communication is not simple. ____________________

   More communication is not always better. ____________________

   Communication will not solve all problems. ____________________

Communication is not always a good thing. ______________________________

____

PART 3

INSTRUCTIONS:

1. For each principle listed below, can you think of ways that our pop culture, current events, and/or society at large imply the **opposite** of these is true? Why do you think it might be appealing to believe the opposite?

   Meanings rest in people, not words. When lawyers, or others, state that something that was said wa unequivocal, they fail to recognize that individuals can still attach their own meaning (decode) to messages (words), implying the meaning is in the words, not in the people.

   Communication does not require complete understanding. ______________________________

   ____

   ____

   Communication is not simple. ______________________________

   ____

   ____

   More communication is not always better. ______________________________

   ____

   ____

   Communication will not solve all problems. ______________________________

   ____

   ____

   Communication is not always a good thing. ______________________________

   ____

   ____

   Communication is not simple. ______________________________

   ____

   ____

   No single person or event causes another's reaction. ______________________________

   ____

   Meanings rest in people, not words. ______________________________

   ____

NAME ______________________

HAPTER 1. ACTIVITY 4: CHARACTERISTICS OF COMPETENT COMMUNICATORS

JRPOSES:

1. To evaluate your own communication behaviors with regard to characteristics of competent communicators.
2. To identify ways in which communication competence can be developed.

ISTRUCTIONS:

1. For each of the six items listed below, rate yourself from 1–5. You might want to ask a close friend to rate you also, as her perception may remind you of strengths you've displayed.
2. Then comment on your own behaviors with regard to each factor by giving an example of why you rated yourself as you did or of your thoughts or feelings with regard to your rating. Then describe what you think you can do to enhance your competence with regard to that factor.

1 = I do not possess this characteristic to any degree.
2 = I have seen this characteristic in myself on rare occasions.
3 = About half the time, I think I display this characteristic.
4 = Most of the time I think I act in accordance with this characteristic.
5 = This is so much a part of me that I don't even think about it. I display this characteristic continuously in my interaction with others.

1. Competent communicators own a wide range of behaviors rather than just a few.

   Self-rating _______ (optional) Friend's rating _______

   Comments on, reasons for, examples of why this rating was given: ______________________

   ____

   ____

   Ways that I might become more competent with regard to this factor: ______________________

   ____

   ____

2. Competent communicators have the ability to choose the most appropriate behavior.

   Self-rating _______ (optional) Friend's rating _______

   Comments on, reasons for, examples of why this rating was given: ______________________

   ____

   ____

   Ways that I might become more competent with regard to this factor: ______________________

   ____

   ____

3. Competent communicators have the skill at performing behaviors.

Self-rating ______ (optional) Friend's rating ______

Comments on, reasons for, examples of why this rating was given: ______

Ways that I might become more competent with regard to this factor: ______

4. Competent communicators demonstrate empathy and perspective taking.

Self-rating ______ (optional) Friend's rating ______

Comments on, reasons for, examples of why this rating was given: ______

Ways that I might become more competent with regard to this factor: ______

5. Competent communicators employ cognitive complexity.

Self-rating ______ (optional) Friend's rating ______

Comments on, reasons for, examples of why this rating was given: ______

Ways that I might become more competent with regard to this factor: ______

6. Competent communicators exercise self-monitoring.

Self-rating ______ (optional) Friend's rating ______

Comments on, reasons for, examples of why this rating was given: ______

Ways that I might become more competent with regard to this factor: ______

NAME ______________________

HAPTER 1. ACTIVITY 5: EXPLORING THE WEB

ROFESSIONAL COMMUNICATION ASSOCIATIONS

he study of communication, like the study of any other academic subject, may seem overwhelming to a ginning student. Five types of communication (intrapersonal, interpersonal, group, public, mass) are scribed in Chapter One, yet there are many more facets to the communication discipline. One way to t an overview of the field of communication is to look at the Web sites of professional organizations in mmunication.

Some of the major professional organizations are

merican Communication Association (ACA) *http://www.americancomm.org*

ternational Communication Association (ICA) *http://www.icahdq.org/index.html*

ational Communication Association (NCA) *http://www.natcom.org*

orld Communication Association (WCA) *http://ilc2.doshisha.ac.jp/users/kkitao/organi/wca/*

1. Go to the NCA Web site. List ten or more types of communication categories by looking at the divisions and commissions. (Go to "About NCA" and the "Unit Affiliations" for a complete list.)

______________________ ______________________

______________________ ______________________

______________________ ______________________

______________________ ______________________

______________________ ______________________

______________________ ______________________

2. If you were to continue your study of communication, which divisions would you most want to know more of? Why?

____

____

3. Are there any categories of communication that you would expect to find and don't? If so, which?

____

____

____

4. In your own words, state the purpose of the NCA.

____

____

5. Compare and contrast the purpose of the NCA with that of either the WCA or the ACA.

6. How closely are the divisions discussed in your text reflected in the divisions of the NCA?

7. If the criterion used to evaluate the Web sites is usefulness for beginning communication students, which of these four organizational sites is best? Give reasons for your answer.

8. Can you find other professional communication Web sites? Here are the names of some that you might find by using a search engine: Eastern Communication Association, Southern Communication Association, Central States Communication Association, and Western States Communication Association. (Hint: From the Western site at *http://www.csufresno.edu/speechcomm/wscalink.htm,* look for (and click on) LINKS TO FRIENDLY COMMUNICATION HOMEPAGES. From there you will be able to find the others, plus many state associations and other national associations.)

Web sites for

ECA ____________________

SSCA ____________________

WSCA ____________________

CSCA ____________________

Your own state association ____________________

NAME ______________________________

HAPTER 1 SELF TEST

ATCHING (KEY TERMS)

atch each term listed on the left with its correct definition from the column on the right.

_____ **1.** small group communication
_____ **2.** messages
_____ **3.** sender
_____ **4.** dyadic communication
_____ **5.** channel
_____ **6.** encoding
_____ **7.** intrapersonal communication
_____ **8.** linear model
_____ **9.** feedback
_____ **10.** inclusion
_____ **11.** external noise
_____ **12.** physiological noise
_____ **13.** decoding
_____ **14.** transactional model
_____ **15.** communication
_____ **16.** communication competence
_____ **17.** noise
_____ **18.** social need
_____ **19.** mass communication
_____ **20.** environment

a. medium through which a message passes
b. continuous, irreversible process in which persons are simultaneously sending and receiving messages
c. source of message
d. process in which receiver attaches meaning to message
e. a response to another message
f. process of putting thoughts into symbols, which are frequently words
g. physical setting and personal perspectives involved in the communication process
h. factors outside the communicators, such as blaring radios and hot temperatures, that interfere with accurate reception of a message
i. a need to be involved in and a part of other groups
j. communication defined by the number of persons (involves two people)
k. communication that occurs within a single person
l. characterization of communication as a one-way event with messages going from sender to receiver
m. symbolic behavior presented to a large audience, through a medium, with delayed or restricted feedback
n. planned and unplanned words and nonverbal behaviors that others attach meanings to
o. external, physiological, and psychological distractions that interfere with a message
p. biological factors that interfere with accurate communication
q. communication in which each person can actively participate with the others in the group
r. identified by Maslow as needs associated with interpersonal relationships
s. communication shown as simultaneous sending and receiving of messages in an ongoing, irreversible process
t. ability to maintain a relationship on terms acceptable to all parties

MULTIPLE CHOICE

Choose the BEST response from those listed.

1. The way interpersonal communication is used in this text

a. includes all human, animal, and mechanical communication.
b. includes communion, as used in a religious sense.
c. includes radio and television programming.
d. includes all of the above.
e. includes none of the above.

2. "Communication is a process" means that

a. communication has clear beginning and ending points.
b. communication resembles still pictures more than motion pictures.
c. communication is ongoing and continuous.
d. communication consists of discrete and separate acts.
e. all of the above

3. The same behavior in two different contexts may be perceived as competent in one setting and incompetent in another. This situation best illustrates the concept that communication competence

a. is not situational.
b. involves conflict.
c. requires cognitive complexity.
d. involves choosing the most appropriate behavior.
e. all of the above

4. Journaling (keeping a private journal in which you write down your feelings and thoughts for only you to read) is an example of

a. dyadic communication.
b. intrapersonal communication.
c. mass communication.
d. interpersonal communication.
e. public communication.

5. Which of these is dyadic communication?

a. two sisters arguing
b. a husband and wife making plans for the weekend
c. a coach and player discussing last week's game
d. an editor and a reporter hammering out an outline for an article
e. all of the above

6. An example of self-monitoring is

a. videotaping your practice interview.
b. carrying a checklist to remind you of some skills to practice.
c. paying attention to the sound of your voice.
d. watching others react to your joke telling.
e. all of the above

7. When we say that communicators occupy different environments, we mean that
   a. one might be rich and one poor.
   b. one might be from China and one from the U.S.
   c. one might be retired with time on her hands, while one is rushing to meet family and career demands with never enough time.
   d. that one has been at a company for ten years and one has just been hired.
   e. All of the above represent differing environments.

8. A plane flying overhead and interfering with your conversation is an example of _________ noise.
   a. external
   b. physiological
   c. psychological
   d. all of the above
   e. none of the above

9. An instructor is lively and joking in a class which comes prepared and always does more than the assigned tasks. The same instructor is strict and unyielding in a class that tries to slide by with minimal work and comes without having read assignments. Although this is the same instructor, the communication behavior illustrates the concept of
   a. all communication is equally effective and competent.
   b. communication is linear.
   c. communication is static.
   d. communication is transactional and relational.
   e. none of the above

10. Symbols
   a. stand for something other than themselves.
   b. represent ideas, but not people, things, or events.
   c. mean exactly the same thing to various people.
   d. are not arbitrary; all symbols have logical reasons for their existence.
   e. have nothing to do with verbal communication.

11. The instructor dislikes the picture of the rock group on your shirt. Her attitude toward the group leads the instructor to experience _________ noise.
   a. external
   b. physiological
   c. psychological
   d. all of the above
   e. none of the above

12. You have an auditory processing difficulty and cannot always understand directions when they are spoken too quickly. You experience _________ noise.
   a. external
   b. physiological
   c. psychological
   d. all of the above
   e. none of the above

13. Your friend asks to borrow your car. Recently, you've had car problems and have been bombarded by other friends with requests to use your car. You're not feeling well and just want to go home. You respond angrily to your friend's request, although on other occasions this particular friend has borrowed your car with no problems. Your reaction this time seems to best illustrate the principle that

a. communication will not solve all problems.
b. no single person or event causes a reaction.
c. communication does not always require understanding.
d. more communication is not always better.
e. competent communicators don't yell.

14. Which statement is accurate regarding communication competence?

a. It is situational.
b. You either have it or you don't.
c. For any situation, there is one ideal way to communicate.
d. Competence requires meeting one goal at the expense of another.
e. None of the above is true.

15. In most situations, competent communicators will

a. be able to choose from a wide range of behaviors.
b. demonstrate empathy.
c. demonstrate skill at a chosen behavior.
d. employ self-monitoring behaviors.
e. all of the above

16. Which type of noise is represented by having a stuffy nose, allergy congestion, and a sore throat?

a. physical
b. external
c. physiological
d. psychological
e. none of the above

17. This is best described as which type of model? s → r [s = sender, r = receiver]

a. linear
b. transactional
c. interpersonal
d. all of the above
e. none of the above

TRUE/FALSE

Circle the T or F to indicate whether you believe the statement is true or false. If it is **true**, give a **reason** or an **example**. If it is **false**, **explain** what would make it true.

T F **1.** According to the text, there is little research to suggest a connection between communication skills and physical health.

____

____

T F **2.** Linear models offer the best hope for understanding the complexity of communication.

____

____

T F **3.** Computer-mediated communication such as e-mail illustrates that quality communication can occur online.

____

____

T F **4.** Interpersonal communication must be face-to-face.

____

____

T F **5.** If you are very good at a particular communication skill, you should probably choose to use that skill in most situations, rather than trying to choose new skills for various contexts.

____

____

COMPLETION

Fill in each of the blanks with a word from the lists provided. Choose the BEST word for each sentence. There are more words than you will use, but each word will be used only once.

message	**control**	**transactional**	**feedback**
noise	**social**		

1. This C←→C (c = communicator) represents a/an ____________________ model of communication.

2. Anything that interferes with effective communication is called ____________________.

3. A/an ____________________ is any stimulus that other people create meaning from, for instance, your hair color.

4. A nod or smile in response to someone saying "hello" to you would be called ____________________.

5. A need to be with other people and have interpersonal relationships is identified by Maslow as a/an ____________________ need.

CHAPTER 1 ANSWERS TO SELF TEST

MATCHING (KEY TERMS)

1. q	**2.** n	**3.** c	**4.** j	**5.** a
6. f	**7.** k	**8.** l	**9.** e	**10.** i
11. h	**12.** p	**13.** d	**14.** s	**15.** b
16. t	**17.** o	**18.** r	**19.** m	**20.** g

MULTIPLE CHOICE

1. e	**2.** c	**3.** d	**4.** b	**5.** e
6. e	**7.** e	**8.** a	**9.** d	**10.** a
11. c	**12.** b	**13.** b	**14.** a	**15.** e
16. c	**17.** a			

TRUE/FALSE

1. False	**2.** False	**3.** True	**4.** False	**5.** False

COMPLETION

1. transactional	**2.** noise	**3.** message	**4.** feedback	**5.** social

RELATED READING

"Shyness: The Behavior of Not Communicating," from (Chapter 3) *Communication: Apprehension, Avoidance, and Effectiveness,* 4th ed., Virginia P. Richmond and James C. McCroskey (Gorsuch Scarisbrick, 1995).

PREVIEW:

Who cannot identify with feeling shy at some point? If, as this chapter indicates, 80% of us at some point (possibly now) have considered ourselves shy, then most of us will find this article engaging. Virginia P. Richmond and James C. McCroskey are renowned communication scholars, researchers, and writers. In this chapter from their book on communication apprehension, they delve into the concept of shyness and the communication implications of that behavior. You will see how choosing not to communicate verbally may result in your communicating to others messages that you may not intend. The scales in the book include an Introversion, a Shyness, and a Willingness to Communicate scale. Also included is a Personal Report of Communication Apprehension measure, which gives you an overview of your level of apprehension in key areas addressed in this text: group discussion, interpersonal conversation, and public speaking situations. You will find these scales an interesting way to initiate your study of communication. As you explore the correlation between communication and the nature and causes of shyness, the types of shy people, and the measures of shyness, you may discover new ways to relate the material in the text to your individual needs.

REVIEW:

1. What kinds of comments (like those in paragraph three) do you think people make about you with regard to effectiveness of, amount of, and desire for communication?
2. How would you rate yourself on these continuums:

   ineffective communicator——————————————— effective communicator

   talks little——————————————————————— talks a lot

   not very willing to communicate————————————— willing to communicate

3. What do you think of the authors' contention that it usually isn't talking too much that creates a negative impression but not having something deemed worthwhile to say?
4. How could you "translate" the concepts in this article into general advice for students with regard to appropriate classroom participation?
5. In what ways have your attempts to communicate been met with "inconsistent reinforcement"?
6. What do you think played a greater role in your learning to communicate: genetics, modeling, or reinforcement?

NOTES ON HUMAN COMMUNICATION: WHAT AND WHY

Chapter 2
Perception, the Self, and Communication

FTER STUDYING THIS CHAPTER, YOU WILL BETTER UNDERSTAND:

1. How common perceptual tendencies and situational factors influence perception.
2. The influence of culture on perception and the self-concept.
3. The importance of empathy in improving communication.
4. The communicative influences that shape the self-concept.
5. How self-fulfilling prophecies can influence behavior.
6. How the process of identity management can result in presentation of multiple selves.
7. The reasons for identity management, and the ethical dimensions of presenting multiple faces.

FTER STUDYING THIS CHAPTER, YOU WILL BE BETTER ABLE TO:

1. Identify how the perceptual tendencies listed in this chapter have led you to develop distorted perceptions of others and yourself.
2. Use perception checking to be more accurate in your perceptions of others' behavior.
3. Identify the ways you influence the self-concepts of others and the ways significant others influence your self-concept.
4. Identify the communication-related self-fulfilling prophecies that you have imposed on yourself, that others have imposed on you, and that you have imposed on others.
5. Describe the various impressions you attempt to create, and discuss the ethical merit of your identity management strategies.

HAPTER 2 SKELETON OUTLINE

his outline can be a helpful study tool to assist you in seeing the order and sequence of the chapter and e relationship of ideas. Use it to take notes as you read and/or to add concepts presented in lecture.

I. **PERCEIVING OTHERS IS AN ACTIVITY INFLUENCED BY PERCEPTUAL TENDENCIES, SITUATIONAL FACTORS, CULTURE, AND OUR ABILITY AND WILLINGNESS TO EMPATHIZE.**
   - A. Common perceptual tendencies
     1. Judging ourselves more charitably
     2. Being influenced by the most obvious stimuli
        - a. intense
        - b. repetitious
        - c. contrasting
        - d. motives
     3. Clinging to first impressions
     4. Assuming others are similar to us
     5. Favoring negative impressions
     6. Blaming the victims
   - B. Situational factors
     1. Relational satisfaction

2. Degree of involvement
3. Past experience
4. Expectations
5. Knowledge
6. Self-concept

C. Culture influences perception.
1. What we select to notice
2. How we interpret nonverbal behavior
3. Value placed on talk and silence
4. Geography

D. Empathy is related to perception and can aid effective communication.
1. Empathy
a. perspective taking
b. emotional dimension
c. concern
d. differs from sympathy, which involves compassion, not identification
2. A three-part **perception check** helps discern perception's accuracy.
a. description of behavior
b. two different but possible interpretations
c. request for clarification
d. congruent nonverbal behavior

II. SELF-CONCEPT INFLUENCES PERCEPTION AND COMMUNICATION

A. Self-concept (define)

B. Reflected appraisal by significant others

C. Culture, language, and values influence self-concept.
1. Collectivism and individualism influence values.
a. collectivism
b. individualism
2. Each emphasizes and rewards different behaviors and self-perceptions.

D. The self-concept ties to personality and communication.
1. Personality (define)
2. Contextual variations affect behavior, interpretation, personality, and communication.

E. Self-fulfilling prophecy (define)
1. What you tell yourself
2. What another tells you

III. IDENTITY MANAGEMENT (IMPRESSION MANAGEMENT) IS THE USE OF COMMUNICATION TO TRY TO MANAGE THE IMPRESSIONS OTHERS HAVE OF US.

A. Public and private selves can be broken into perceived and presenting selves.
1. Perceived self (define)
2. The presenting self (define)
3. Much behavior is an attempt to manage impressions.
4. Effectiveness and competence
a. high self-monitors
b. low self-monitors
c. flexible communicators

B. Reasons we manage impressions
1. Social rules/situations
2. Personal goals

C. Impression management occurs in face-to-face and mediated contexts.
1. Face-to-face impression management occurs through manner, appearance, and setting.
2. Mediated has advantages and disadvantages for impression management.

D. Impression management involves issues of honesty.
1. Honest or dishonest
2. Choice of faces and impressions

HAPTER 2 KEY TERMS

'his list of key terms corresponds to those in boldface in your text. Use these lines to write the efinition and/or an example of the word on the line next to it.

ttribution ______________________________

____

mpathy ______________________________

____

ce ______________________________

____

cework ______________________________

____

npression management ______________________________

____

rceived self ______________________________

____

rception checking ______________________________

____

rsonality ______________________________

____

esenting self ______________________________

____

flected appraisal ______________________________

____

lf-concept ______________________________

____

self-fulfilling prophecy ______________________________

____

self-serving bias ______________________________

____

significant other ______________________________

____

NAME ______________________________

CHAPTER 2. ACTIVITY 1: PERCEPTUAL TENDENCIES

PURPOSE:

1. To identify common perceptual tendencies in specific instances.

INSTRUCTIONS:

1. Common perceptual tendencies often distort our perception of others. Being able to recognize when this is occurring can help improve communication. Read the following situational descriptions.
2. For each, identify which of the following perceptual tendencies is illustrated.
   - **A.** Judging ourselves more charitably than others, thus perceiving similar behavior from others and ourselves differently.
   - **B.** Being influenced by what is most obvious, including stimuli that are intense, repetitious, contrasting, or related to our motives.
   - **C.** Clinging to first impressions, even if they're wrong.
   - **D.** Assuming others are similar to us in attitudes and motives.
   - **E.** Favoring negative impressions over positive ones.
   - **F.** Blaming innocent victims for their misfortunes.

Example:

A 13-year-old is hit and killed by a car speeding through a red light at 1:30 a.m. A person wonders aloud, "What in the world was she doing out at 1:30 in the morning? She should have been home."

F We tend to blame victims, in this case the teen, and act like it is her fault, instead of blaming the driver for speeding and running a red light.

1. You are trying to pay attention to a friend who is talking to you, but you're worried about your child falling from the playground equipment.

   ____

2. A child brings home a report card with six A's and a D. The parents first want to know why the child is getting a D.

   ____

3. The story is told of a woman sitting next to a man on an airplane. He said, "I just got out of prison for murdering my wife." "Oh," she replied, "then you're single."

   ____

4. A parent (who married at age 20): "My son is so young to be dating seriously. He's only 20 and not very mature and already talking marriage with his girlfriend."

   ____

5. You thought a new co-worker was trying to juggle the schedule to get the best days and time off at your expense. You later learn that he didn't know the procedure to sign up for scheduling, but still are suspicious of the person.

   ____

6. A person is attacked and robbed in a particular neighborhood. Others comment, "He should have known better than to walk through that area."

Add your own examples:

1.

2.

3.

NAME ____________________

HAPTER 2. ACTIVITY 2: CULTURE AND PERCEPTION

URPOSES:

1. To discover the ways in which culture influences our selection and perception.
2. To illustrate the variety of ways our interpretations are influenced by culture.

ART 1

NSTRUCTIONS:

erception and culture are closely related; culture teaches us how to perceive and strongly influences ur selection of what to pay attention to, our interpretation of nonverbal behavior, and the value we lace on talk and silence.

1. For each proverb, write down your own impressions of what it tells us about communication behaviors that are and are not valued. If you repeatedly heard this proverb, what would you select to pay attention to when communicating with someone? How would you interpret others' verbal and nonverbal behavior? How would exposure to this proverb and its cultural values influence the way you communicate with others?
2. Then, discuss with others what your impressions were, how similar or different they are, and whether these proverbs or similar ones were familiar to you.

xample:

e who speaks does not know; he who knows does not speak. (Chinese)

omeone who hears this proverb would believe that the person who talks a lot doesn't really know uch. The person with wisdom would be the silent one. A person would pay attention to a quiet person nd ignore loud, boisterous, outgoing people, judging them to be ignorant.

e who raises his voice first, loses. (Chinese) ____________________

____

____

he squeaky wheel gets the grease. ____________________

____

____

oud thunder brings little rain (Chinese) [contrast to previous one] ____________________

____

____

eauty is only skin deep. ____________________

____

____

urn your face to the sun and the shadows fall behind you. (Maori) ____________________

____

____

Blood is thicker than water. ______________________________

____

____

Life is a dance, not a race. (Irish) ______________________________

____

____

You can catch more flies with honey than with vinegar. ______________________________

____

____

Silence is golden; speech is silver. ______________________________

____

____

All's well that ends well. ______________________________

____

____

Cleanliness is next to godliness. ______________________________

____

____

Order is half of life. (German) ______________________________

____

____

The mouth maintains silence in order to hear the heart talk. (Belgian) ______________________________

____

____

Nothing done with intelligence is done without speech. (Greek, from Isocrates) ______________________________

____

____

The eyes are the window to the soul. ______________________________

____

____

ART 2

hat proverbs are popular in your culture to remind members of appropriate verbal and nonverbal ommunication behaviors? List some proverbs or sayings you frequently heard while growing up and escribe how they influence your perception and communication. If there are students in class or if you ave friends who speak languages other than English, ask them to think of proverbs in other languages nd try to translate and explain them for you.

roverb: ______________________________

____

xplanation and impact on communication. ______________________________

____

____

roverb: ______________________________

____

xplanation and impact on communication. ______________________________

____

____

iscuss these last proverbs and determine if they reinforce collectivism or individualism. What ehaviors would be rewarded? What behaviors would be rebuked?

he nail that stands out must be pounded down. (Japan) ______________________________

____

____

he early bird gets the worm. ______________________________

____

____

single arrow is easily broken, but not a bunch. (Asian) ______________________________

____

____

od helps those who help themselves. ______________________________

____

____

NOTES ON PERCEPTION, THE SELF, AND COMMUNICATION

NAME ______________________

CHAPTER 2. ACTIVITY 3: PERCEPTION CHECKS

PURPOSES:

1. To become familiar with the parts of the perception check.
2. To develop competence in identifying ways to use perception checks.
3. To develop skills in creating appropriate perception checks.

INSTRUCTIONS:

1. Read each situation below and think about various perceptions of the event.
2. Create a three-part **perception check** to help you discern whether your perceptions are accurate. Write it as you would actually say it to the other person. Be sure to include
   a. a description of behavior
   b. two possible, but different, interpretations of the behavior
   c. a request for clarification of how to interpret the behavior
3. Now, role play with a classmate. Practice delivering your perception check with the appropriate nonverbal delivery skills to reflect a sincere attempt to understand.
4. Finally, consider whether you actually would use a perception check in each situation. Why or why not?

1. For the last three evenings you've come home and found your neighbor's car (Apt 2) parked in your space (marked Apt 3).

   Describe the behavior. ______________________

   ____

   One interpretation ______________________

   ____

   Second, different, but possible interpretation ______________________

   ____

   Request for clarification ______________________

   ____

   Nonverbal behaviors I would/wouldn't display ______________________

   ____

2. You wanted two California rolls, so you inquired how many come with an order. You asked for one order (two pieces) of California rolls. Two orders (two plates/four rolls) are delivered to your table.

   Describe the behavior. ______________________

   ____

   One interpretation ______________________

   ____

   Second, different, but possible interpretation ______________________

   ____

Request for clarification ______________________________

____

Nonverbal behaviors I would/wouldn't display ______________________________

____

3. You and your spouse agreed not to write checks until after deposits are made. You go to the checkbook (joint account) and find a space left for a deposit but no amount written in and two checks written out without funds.

Describe the behavior. ______________________________

____

One interpretation ______________________________

____

Second, different, but possible interpretation ______________________________

____

Request for clarification ______________________________

____

Nonverbal behaviors I would/wouldn't display ______________________________

____

4. A group of six of you eat at a restaurant. You noticed that the menu indicated that a 20% tip will automatically be added to groups of eight or more. When the bill comes, a 20% charge is added in.

Describe the behavior. ______________________________

____

One interpretation ______________________________

____

Second, different, but possible interpretation ______________________________

____

Request for clarification ______________________________

____

Nonverbal behaviors I would/wouldn't display ______________________________

____

5. A certain bookstore gives a 10% discount to students. You show your ID for your purchase of a book on sale for $18.00. The clerk rings up $18.00 plus tax and tells you the total.

Describe the behavior. ______________________________

____

One interpretation ______________________________

____

Second, different, but possible interpretation ______________________________

____

Request for clarification ______________________________

____

Nonverbal behaviors I would/wouldn't display ______________________________

____

6. You are new in an office. You know about a party Friday night at Joe's house because several other co-workers (not Joe) include you in conversations as if you are invited. You never received an invitation, and you don't know if the invitations are just word of mouth and it's understood that all are invited, or if only certain people are invited.

Describe the behavior. ______________________________

____

One interpretation ______________________________

____

Second, different, but possible interpretation ______________________________

____

Request for clarification ______________________________

____

Nonverbal behaviors I would/wouldn't display ______________________________

____

Now, divide the situations (by number) into those in which you probably would use a perception check and those you wouldn't. For each group, discuss the advantages and disadvantages and the probable results of using or not using perception checks.

Numbers of situations in which I probably would use a perception check: ________

Advantages and probable results of using perception checks ________________________________

____

____

____

Possible disadvantages ____

____

____

Numbers of situations in which I probably would not use a perception check: ________

Disadvantages and probable results of using perception checks ______________________________

____

____

____

Possible advantages ____

____

____

NAME ______________________________

CHAPTER 2. ACTIVITY 4: IDENTITY MANAGEMENT

PURPOSES:

1. To understand how identity management (impression management) is used to create or maintain a presenting self.
2. To practice creative thinking with regard to ways to manage impressions.

INSTRUCTIONS:

1. For each situation below, describe ways in which you have tried or would try to manage impressions.
2. For each situation tell which reason was behind the impression: to follow situational social rules and to meet personal goals, such as appearing likeable, responsible, or competent.
3. Now go back to your description of what you did or would do and label the items to indicate which were accomplished through **manner** (words, nonverbal actions), **appearance** (clothing, make-up, hair), and **setting** (briefcase, car, type of furniture, music, color, computer).
4. After reflecting on the categories in #3, are there additional ways you believe would be an improvement in managing impressions?

Example:

You have been invited to a new co-worker's home for a backyard barbecue.

What would you or did you do? Probably wear something in denim, but nicer than just jeans and a tee-shirt. Perhaps a blazer with jeans, so the blazer could be removed if others were more casual. I'd see if the host was doing introductions. If not, I'd greet everyone and introduce myself to those I'd seen at work but didn't really know.

Reason for managing impression I'd want to be polite and show respect by dressing appropriately, not so "dressed up" that it looked like I was showing off, not torn or dirty or such informal clothes that they'd think I didn't care. I'd want to create a friendly impression since I'm new at work.

Ways in which impression management was done (label items manner, appearance, setting)

Additional ways you would manage impressions:

manner smiles, moving around among people if that's what others are doing

appearance nothing real showy or revealing. Depending on the region of the country, I'd think about cowboy boots or shorts.

setting I'd ask if I should bring some food or drinks, as that's the custom in some places.

1. Job interview. [You decide the type of job: ______________________________]

   What would you or did you do? ______________________________

   ____

   ____

   Reason for managing impression ______________________________

   ____

Ways in which impression management was done (label items manner, appearance, setting)

Additional ways you would manage impressions:

manner ____________________

appearance ____________________

setting ____________________

2. First day of class and you want to create an impression of ____________________

What would you or did you do? ____________________

____

____

Reason for managing impression ____________________

____

Ways in which impression management was done (label items manner, appearance, setting)

Additional ways you would manage impressions:

manner ____________________

appearance ____________________

setting ____________________

3. Dinner with your boyfriend/girlfriend's family and you want them to like you.

What would you or did you do? ____________________

____

____

Reason for managing impression ____________________

____

Ways in which impression management was done (label items manner, appearance, setting)

Additional ways you would manage impressions:

manner ____________________

appearance ____________________

setting ____________________

4. Appearing in court to seek dismissal of a traffic violation.

What would you or did you do? ______________________________

____

____

Reason for managing impression ______________________________

____

Ways in which impression management was done (label items manner, appearance, setting)

Additional ways you would manage impressions:

manner ______________________________

appearance ______________________________

setting ______________________________

5. Challenge: You want to impress someone on the Internet whom you've never met. [I'd like to make this kind of impression: ______________________________]

What would you or did you do? ______________________________

____

____

Reason for managing impression ______________________________

____

Do any of the ways fit these categories? (manner, appearance, setting)

Besides those three, are there additional channels (not available in face-to-face) available to you on Web pages? In chat rooms? In list-serve discussions? ______________________________

____

____

In using the Internet channels, what are the advantages you gain in terms of impression management? What would you or did you do? ______________________________

____

____

What disadvantages do you need to contend with? ____________________

____

____

Besides Internet channels, what other mediums or channels have you used that have presented you with distinct advantages or disadvantages in terms of managing impressions? ____________________

____

____

____

____

NAME ______________________

CHAPTER 2. ACTIVITY 5: SELF-CONCEPT AND COMMUNICATION

PURPOSE:

1. To explore one's self-concept and the role of communication in forming self-concept and influencing perception.

INSTRUCTIONS:

Perceiving the self involves understanding self-concept and its impact on communication. Self-concept is defined as the relatively stable set of perceptions we hold about our physical, social, and psychological traits.

1. List several characteristics that are significant in your self-concept. Try to choose some characteristics that are physical, emotional, psychological, and social.
2. Describe the role of communication in forming this part of your self-concept.
3. Then, describe some ways in which that characteristic affects how you communicate with others.

Describe or draw a trait that is part of your self-concept here:	**What was communicated to you? How?** How did communication play a role in your believing yourself to be this way? Did you learn these things about yourself directly or indirectly from others (from direct communication to you or from others' feedback or reactions to you)?	**What do you communicate to others?** How does this trait affect who you communicate with? For what reasons? How you communicate with others? How much you communicate?
Example: I'm shy around new people and I'm not comfortable meeting new people.	When I was young, my older sister was always invited to talk to guests, and introduce them to others. I watched, but believed I wasn't good at this. Others probably paid more attention to my sister because she spoke with them.	Sometimes, I really have to talk myself into approaching new people and I may not be the one to walk up to strangers and start a conversation. I'll wait for someone to start talking to me first.

NAME ________________________________

CHAPTER 2. ACTIVITY 6. EXPLORING THE WEB

IMPRESSION MANAGEMENT

Chapter 2 discusses various aspects of impression management. Read the following articles:

http://www.ntu.ac.uk/soc/psych/miller/goffman.htm Miller, Hugh. "The Presentation of Self in Electronic Life: Goffman on the Internet"

http://www.aber.ac.uk/~dgc/webident.html Chandler, Daniel. "Personal Home Pages and the Construction of Identities on the Web"

If you have your own Web page, answer the following questions with regard to your own home page. If not, use either your instructor's page or the page of a friend or famous person you admire.

I will use ______ my own site ______ a friend's site ______ instructor's site ______ celebrity site

URL ____

1. What evidence does Chandler cite to support his claim that home pages represent a blurring of private and public arenas?

____

____

____

____

____

2. Chandler refers to five elements present in construction of Web pages: inclusion of certain elements, ____________ to particular elements, ____________ of certain elements, ____________ or borrowing of elements (by addition, deletion, substitution, or transposition), and ____________ of the elements on a Web page.

3. Describe how each of the five underlined elements relates to the person's Web page you're analyzing.

____

____

____

____

____

4. Define *bricolage*. Explain Chandler's use of the term *bricolage* as it relates to the Web page you're analyzing.

____

____

____

____

5. Analyze the content and form of the Web page you are examining. What do you find appealing or unappealing about its content? About its form?

____

____

____

6. Does the page have any of these: guest book, e-mail capacity, chat link? What does the presence or absence of these contribute to the Web-identity of the person?

____

____

____

Review these sites for more information about analyzing Web pages and their design:

http://www.wilsonweb.com/articlees/12design.htm

http://www.werbach.com/web/page_design.html

NAME ______________________________

CHAPTER 2 SELF TEST

MATCHING (KEY TERMS)

_____ 1. attribution

_____ 2. empathy

_____ 3. face

_____ 4. facework

_____ 5. impression management

_____ 6. perceived self

_____ 7. perception checking

_____ 8. personality

_____ 9. presenting self

_____ 10. reflected appraisal

_____ 11. self-concept

_____ 12. self-fulfilling prophecy

_____ 13. self-serving bias

_____ 14. significant other

a. tendency to interpret and explain information in a way that casts the perceiver in the most favorable manner
b. person whose opinion is important enough to a person to strongly affect his or her self-concept
c. theory that a person's self-concept matches the way the person believes others regard him or her
d. the process of attaching meaning to behavior
e. ability to project oneself into another's point of view, to experience that person's thoughts and feelings
f. a three-part method for verifying the accuracy of one's perception of another
g. the socially approved identity that a communicator tries to present
h. communication strategies used to influence others' views of oneself
i. the relatively stable set of perceptions a person has of himself or herself
j. the person a communicator believes, in candid moments, that he or she is
k. verbal and nonverbal behavior to create and maintain communicator's and others' face
l. the image a person presents to others
m. a relatively consistent set of traits a person exhibits across a variety of situations
n. a prediction or expectation of an event that makes the outcome more likely to occur than would otherwise have been the case

MULTIPLE CHOICE

Choose the BEST response from those listed.

1. Perception checks include all EXCEPT

   a. a description of behavior observed.
   b. a request for clarification.
   c. a statement of intent—how you will treat the person in the future.
   d. use of objective words to describe behavior.
   e. appropriate nonverbal behaviors.

2. In her book, *First Ladies,* Margaret Truman writes, "When Ronald Reagan was seriously wounded by a would-be assassin in 1981, Nancy Reagan received a deeply compassionate letter from Jacqueline Kennedy Onassis, who knew, better than any living former First Lady, the terror and grief and anguish such an experience evokes. Later, Jackie followed up the letter with a phone call. Nancy never forgot this . . . and expressed her enduring gratitude for it when Jackie died of cancer in 1994." In this case, it seems that Jackie communicated so well because she demonstrated

   a. empathy.
   b. facework.
   c. self-serving bias.
   d. sympathy.
   e. attribution.

3. When a person's car is stolen after being left unlocked in front of his home, a neighbor is heard to say, "He should have known better. He should lock his car." When the neighbor's car was subsequently stolen, she commented, "The police aren't doing their job protecting us. We should be safe in our own neighborhoods. They need to be tougher on crime." The woman's attitude toward the first theft indicates which perceptual error?

   a. Favoring negative impressions
   b. Being influenced by the most obvious stimuli
   c. Judging ourselves more charitably
   d. Assuming others are similar to us
   e. Clinging to first impressions

4. "When I see the crumbs all over the counter and dishes stacked in the sink, I don't know if you've got a big exam and have been too busy studying to clean up or if you have time but are hoping that I'll just clean up. What's the reason?" This is an example of a

   a. significant other.
   b. perceived self.
   c. perception check.
   d. reflected appraisal.
   e. self-serving bias.

5. As it is used in this text, a significant other is always someone

   a. with whom you have a romantic involvement.
   b. whose opinion matters to you.
   c. whom you have known since childhood.
   d. who holds the job you aspire to.
   e. whose reflected appraisal of you doesn't matter to you.

6. Two people speak Spanish as a first language and English as a second. With regard to this trait, one has been made fun of for her accent, was punished by teachers in elementary school for speaking Spanish, and feels inferior. The other was always praised by teachers and family for speaking two languages, is happy when co-workers call upon her to translate, and feels proud and accomplished at being bilingual. With regard to their self-concepts, this example illustrates

   a. that having the same traits results in the same or similar self-concepts.
   b. that self-concept consists not only of the traits we possess, but of the significance we attach to them.
   c. that reflected appraisal helps to shape self-concept.
   d. both a and b.
   e. both b and c.

7. Maslow wrote, "If the only tool you have is a hammer, you tend to treat everything as if it were a nail." This statement illustrates

a. attribution.
b. perception.
c. facework.
d. perception checking.
e. impression management.

8. The primary way we develop our self-concepts is through

a. reflections during our solitude.
b. interaction with others.
c. religious beliefs.
d. building defenses against unwanted experiences.
e. none of the above really influences self-concept.

9. "Our thoughts not only reveal what we are; they predict what we will become." —Tozer. This quotation seems to be most closely related to the concept of

a. sympathy.
b. empathy.
c. attribution.
d. significant other.
e. self-fulfilling prophecy.

10. The social science term *self-serving bias* is most closely related to which common perceptual error?

a. judging ourselves more charitably
b. being influenced by the most obvious stimuli
c. clinging to first impressions
d. assuming others are similar to us
e. favoring negative impressions

11. "At Laguna Pueblo in New Mexico, 'Who is your mother?' is an important question. At Laguna, . . . your mother's identity is the key to your own identity. . . . every individual has a place within the universe—human and nonhuman—and that place is defined by clan membership." —P. G. Allen This quotation is describing a/an _________ culture.

a. nonverbal
b. prehistoric
c. individualist
d. collective
e. assertive

12. "In elementary school the skinny kid with glasses may become a 'brain' because he is given that role by his classmates. If he accepts it, he is likely to spend more time on his homework, and thereby verify the impression which his peers have of him."—Thomas M. Scheidel. That scenario is typical of which concept?

a. sympathy
b. empathy
c. attribution
d. significant other
e. self-fulfilling prophecy

13. The perceptual error of being influenced by the most obvious stimuli refers to stimuli that are

a. intense.
b. repetitious.
c. contrasting.
d. in line with our motives.
e. all of the above

14. In many Asian cultures, being very talkative, speaking directly even when you disagree with a person, and not allowing much silence in a conversation would likely be regarded as

a. a very positive sign of a cultured person.
b. a sign of a very intelligent, knowledgeable person.
c. both a and b.
d. insincere, lacking knowledge, and impolite.
e. a sign of belonging to the group.

15. Culture often influences people's perception of

a. the amount of talk considered appropriate.
b. the value placed on silence.
c. whether direct disagreement is positive or negative.
d. whether eye contact is polite and respectful.
e. all of the above

16. Practicing empathy appears to

a. make communication more difficult between people.
b. help persons see more possible reasons for another's behavior.
c. help others be more tolerant of another.
d. both b and c
e. all of the above

17. Which of these is not one of the key types of communication we use to manage impressions?

a. manner
b. setting
c. appearance
d. All of these are types of communication we use to manage impressions.
e. None of these are types of communication we use to manage impressions.

18. Which is likely an example of a self-fulfilling prophecy?

a. A student gets a low grade on a test after hearing the instructor refer to her as a "special needs student.
b. You tell your spouse that you don't want to go to his/her office party because you think his/her co-workers are snobs and you know you won't have a good time. You go and have a lousy time.
c. An employee hears his/her supervisor say, "There's no way he/she will be able to handle the work without computer help." Although he/she had been doing this kind of work without a computer for a long time, the employee feels unable to keep up now.
d. All could be examples of self-fulfilling prophecy.
e. None are likely examples of self-fulfilling prophecy.

9. "A man is hurt not so much by what happens, as by his opinion of what happens." —Montaigne. This statement reflects the concepts relating to the role of ________ in communication.

a. perception
b. self-concept
c. impression management
d. ethics
e. significant others

RUE/FALSE

ircle the T or F to indicate whether you believe the statement is true or false. If it is **true**, give a **reason** r an **example**. If it is **false**, **explain** what would make it true.

F **1.** Common perceptual errors often distort our perception of others, but have little impact on our communication with others.

____

____

F **2.** Culture teaches us how to perceive and strongly influences our interpretation of nonverbal behavior.

____

____

F **3.** Empathy and sympathy are essentially the same.

____

____

F **4.** A perception check is a way for you to get others to understand your point of view.

____

____

F **5.** Our behavior and our interpretation of behavior affect our communication.

____

____

OMPLETION

ll in each of the blanks with a word from the list provided. Choose the BEST word for each sentence. here are more words than you will use, but each word will be used only once.

npathy	**perception checks**	**self-fulfilling prophecies**
ılture	**selective**	**impression management**

1. Our perceptions of others are always ____________________.

2. A valuable tool for understanding others is increased ____________________.

3. To see whether our interpretations of others' behaviors are accurate, we can use ______________.

4. Deciding which face to display in public is the process of ____________________.

5. Communication and ____________________ shape our self-concepts.

6. Self-concepts may lead us to create ____________________ which result in our acting as if certain beliefs about ourselves were true.

CHAPTER 2. ANSWERS TO SELF TEST

MATCHING (KEY TERMS)

1. d	**2.** e	**3.** l (g)	**4.** k	**5.** h
6. j	**7.** f	**8.** m	**9.** g (l)	**10.** c
11. i	**12.** n	**13.** a	**14.** b	

MULTIPLE CHOICE

1. c	**2.** a	**3.** c	**4.** c	**5.** b
6. e	**7.** b	**8.** b	**9.** e	**10.** a
11. d	**12.** e	**13.** e	**14.** d	**15.** e
16. d	**17.** d	**18.** d	**19.** a	

TRUE/FALSE

1. F	**2.** T	**3.** F	**4.** F	**5.** T

COMPLETION

1. selective	**2.** empathy	**3.** perception checks
4. impression management	**5.** culture	**6.** self-fulfilling prophecies

ELATED READING

Vhite Privilege: Unpacking the Invisible Knapsack," by Peggy McIntosh. Copies and permission to copy n be obtained from Peggy McIntosh, Wellesley College, Mass., 617-283-2520.

REVIEW:

ow is our perception of others influenced by our culture and by our ability and willingness to npathize? Our text describes the key roles culture and empathy play in our perception of and mmunication with others. This provocative article may influence your ideas of "privilege." If you are ot Euroamerican, the article may reflect concepts you've been aware of and tried to articulate. If you e Euroamerican, you may not have given much thought to the unspoken or unacknowledged privileges at you've had in life. Consequently, it may be harder to empathize with others who have not had these ivileges, especially since on the surface, they don't involve large sums of money, great give-aways, or her things that may come to mind when you hear the word *privilege.* The reading may help you see ourself and your privileges as others may see you. Author Peggy McIntosh delves beneath the surface d looks at the subtle advantages that "white" skin has bestowed on its bearers. Ms. McIntosh presents uite a challenge to readers.

EVIEW:

1. If you are Euroamerican, what is your initial reaction to the article? Does the article reflect ways in which you've perceived the privileges of others? Or do you see other, more significant privileges not mentioned?
2. If you are not Euroamerican, does the article reflect ways in which you've perceived the privileges of others? Or do you see other, more significant privileges not mentioned?
3. Why do you think the author uses the metaphor of a knapsack to represent these privileges?
4. Has your perception of privilege been altered by reading this article? How?
5. Has the article made a difference in how you perceive yourself? In how you perceive others?

NOTES ON PERCEPTION, THE SELF, AND COMMUNICATION

Chapter 3
Language

FTER STUDYING THIS CHAPTER, YOU WILL BETTER UNDERSTAND:

1. The symbolic, person-centered nature of language.
2. Phonological, semantic, syntactic, and pragmatic rules which govern language.
3. The ways in which language shapes and reflects perceptions.
4. The types of troublesome language and skills to deal with each.
5. The relationship between language use and gender.
6. The relationship between language and culture.

FTER STUDYING THIS CHAPTER, YOU WILL BE BETTER ABLE TO:

1. Identify at least two ways in which language has shaped your perceptions of a person, an object, an idea, or an event.
2. Identify at least two ways in which your language reflects your attitudes about a person, an object, or an event.
3. Discuss how you and others use syntactic, semantic, phonological, and pragmatic rules and how their use affects a message's comprehension.
4. Recognize and suggest alternatives for equivocal language, relative terms, and overly abstract language.
5. Identify and suggest alternatives for fact–inference and fact–opinion confusion and for emotive statements.
6. Suggest appropriate alternatives for unnecessary or misleading euphemisms and equivocal statements.

HAPTER 3 SKELETON OUTLINE

his outline can be a helpful study tool to assist you in seeing the order and sequence of the chapter and e relationship of ideas. Use it to take notes as you read and/or to add concepts presented in lecture.

I. **THE NATURE OF LANGUAGE**
   A. Symbolic
      1. Elements create symbols (words and other symbols).
      2. Sign language is symbolic, linguistic.
   B. Meanings are in people, not in words.
      1. Meanings are personal.
      2. Dictionary definitions are inadequate in at least three ways.
   C. Rule-governed
      1. Phonological rules
      2. Semantic rules
      3. Syntactic rules
      4. Pragmatic rules
         a. relationship
         b. setting
         c. nonverbal behavior

II. **POWER OF LANGUAGE**
- A. Language shapes attitudes
  - 1. Naming
  - 2. Credibility
  - 3. Status
  - 4. Sexism and racism
- B. Language reflects attitudes
  - 1. Power
  - 2. Affiliation
    - a. convergence and divergence
    - b. attraction and interest
      - (1) demonstrative pronouns
      - (2) negation
      - (3) sequential placement
  - 3. Responsibility
    - a. it vs. I
    - b. you vs. I
    - c. but vs. and
    - d. questions vs. statements

III. **TROUBLESOME LANGUAGE**
- A. The language of misunderstandings
  - 1. Equivocal language
    - a. consequences
    - b. jargon
  - 2. Relative words
  - 3. Slang
  - 4. Jargon
  - 5. Overly abstract language
    - a. abstraction ladder
      - (1) Low-level abstractions are specific.
      - (2) High-level abstractions are generalizations.
        - (a) useful as a shortcut
        - (b) useful to avoid confrontations
        - (c) problematic as stereotyping
        - (d) problematic when confusing to others
    - b. Behavioral descriptions avoid overly abstract language.
      - (1) person(s)—who?
      - (2) circumstances—when and where?
      - (3) observable behaviors—what?
- B. Disruptive language
  - 1. Fact–opinion confusion
    - (a) Facts can be verified.
    - (b) Opinions are beliefs.
  - 2. fact–inference confusion
    - (a) fact
    - (b) inferences/conclusions from interpretations of evidence
  - 3. emotive language
    - (a) denotation
    - (b) connotation
- C. Evasive language
  - 1. Euphemism
  - 2. Equivocation

IV. **GENDER AND LANGUAGE**
- A. Content

B. Reasons for communicating
   1. Women's speech
   2. Men's speech
C. Conversational style
   1. Women's style
   2. Men's style
D. Non-gender variables
   1. Social philosophy
   2. Occupation and social roles
E. Sex roles

CULTURE AND LANGUAGE

A. Verbal communication styles
   1. Directness
      a. low-context cultures
      b. high-context cultures
   2. Elaborate or succinct
      a. Arab elaborated style
      b. succinctness and silence valued
   3. Formality and informality
B. Language and world view
   1. Linguistic determinism
   2. Whorf–Sapir hypothesis
   3. Linguistic relativism
C. Language use in North American culture
   1. Surnames
   2. Ethnic names

APTER 3 KEY TERMS

s list of key terms corresponds to those in boldface in your text. Use these lines to write the inition and/or an example of the word on the line next to it.

tract language ______________________________

____

traction ladder ______________________________

____

avioral description ______________________________

____

notation ______________________________

____

vergence ______________________________

____

denotation ______________________________

____

divergence ______________________________

____

emotive language ______________________________

____

equivocal words ______________________________

____

equivocation ______________________________

____

euphemism ______________________________

____

factual statement ______________________________

____

high-context culture ______________________________

____

inferential statement ______________________________

____

jargon ______________________________

____

language ______________________________

____

linguistic determinism ______________________________

____

linguistic relativism ______________________________

____

low-context culture ______________________________

____

inion statement ______________________________

____

onological rules ______________________________

____

agmatic rules ______________________________

____

lative rules ______________________________

____

mantic rules ______________________________

____

x role ______________________________

____

ang ______________________________

____

ntactic rules ______________________________

____

horf–Sapir hypothesis ______________________________

____

NOTES ON LANGUAGE

NAME ____________________

HAPTER 3. ACTIVITY 1: POWERFUL/POWERLESS LANGUAGE

JRPOSES:

1. To expand understanding of powerless and powerful language
2. To use language which takes rather than avoids responsibility
3. To identify types of powerless language and language lacking in responsibility

ISTRUCTIONS:

1. Read the sentences in the first chart. Identify the type of powerless language used by writing the type of language in the left column. Then rewrite the sentence expressing the idea in more powerful but not rude or offensive language. See Table 3-2. Read the sentences in the second chart. Identify the type of language responsibility problem shown by writing the type of language in the left column. Then rewrite the sentences with language that takes responsibility.

TYPE OF LANGUAGE	POWERLESS	REWRITE USING POWERFUL LANGUAGE
polite forms	*Ms. Smith, I wanted to ask you about the assignment, ma'am.*	*I want to ask about the assignment.*
	There's probably a better way to do this, but let me explain.	
	It was really a good speech.	
	That was a good meeting, wasn't it?	
	I sort of wanted to leave early today.	

TYPE OF LANGUAGE	LACKING RESPONSIBILITY	REWRITE USING RESPONSIBLE LANGUAGE
You vs. I	*You irritate me with your singing in the car.*	*I feel irritated when I'm driving and listening to your singing.*
	There's no reason it won't work, but we don't have the money.	
	Do you think we could go to a Chinese restaurant rather than a pizza place?	
	It's not a good idea.	
	You really get me upset when you drive like that.	

NAME ______________________________

HAPTER 3. ACTIVITY 2: SEXIST AND RELATIVE LANGUAGE

URPOSES:

1. To expand understanding of sexist and relative language.
2. To use nonsexist language and nonrelative words.

ISTRUCTIONS:

1. In the first chart, identify the problem with the language on the left. Then think of other terms that could be substituted.
2. In the second chart, replace the relative word with a nonrelative word that is specific and measurable.

SEXIST LANGUAGE	PROBLEM	REWRITE USING LANGUAGE WHICH DESCRIBES THE FUNCTION
waitress	*Two people doing an identical job have different labels based on sex. Title should describe the job.*	*Server* *Waitperson*
mailman		
master of ceremonies		
"Peace on earth, good will to men."		
"In great matters men show themselves as they wish to be seen; in small matters, as they are." —Gamaliel Bradford		

Change these relative words to more precise language.

USES RELATIVE WORDS	REPLACE RELATIVE WORDS
I'd like a small brownie.	*Make mine no more than one inch square.*
My dad is not very tall.	
I'll be back in a little while.	
Don't make your papers too long or too short.	
I'm a very good student.	

NAME ______________________________

HAPTER 3. ACTIVITY 3: BEHAVIORAL DESCRIPTIONS

RPOSE:

1. To practice replacing abstract statements with behavioral descriptions.

RT 1

STRUCTIONS:

ad the following abstract statements and rewrite each using behavioral descriptions.

ample:

u always get more help from the folks than I do.

ho is involved? Mom

what circumstances? One time, when you couldn't pay your tuition last semester.

hat behaviors are involved? paying tuition for you

earer statement: Mom paid your tuition last semester.

vantages or disadvantages of using the clearer statement: In a discussion with my sister, it limits the ope of what sounds like an attack on her. There is something concrete for her to respond to. The ope of my resentment is narrowed. The "fact" is presented, rather than a vague statement.

pact on you of having to think through the three questions: I had to stop and think of what I really eant and what the "facts" were that I was basing my broad attack on. I had to ask myself what the oblem really was and stop exaggerating it.

, School is so easy for you.

Who is involved? ______________________________

In what circumstances? ______________________________

What behaviors are involved? ______________________________

Clearer statement: ______________________________

Advantages or disadvantages of using the clearer statement: ______________________________

____

Impact on you of having to think through the three questions: ______________________________

____

. The workload around here sure isn't fair.

Who is involved? ______________________________

In what circumstances? ______________________________

What behaviors are involved? ______________________________

Clearer statement: ______________________________

Advantages or disadvantages of using the clearer statement: ______________________________

____

Impact on you of having to think through the three questions: ______________________________

____

PART 2

1. What do you have to do in order to change abstract statements to descriptions?

____

____

2. What effect does this activity have on your thought process?

____

____

3. What effect does this activity have on the time you take to talk to yourself? To express yourself?

____

____

4. Predict what would happen if all abstract speech were converted to behavioral descriptions and other forms of more concrete, specific language. What would happen in personal relationships? government? classrooms? television shows?

____

____

____

NAME ______________________________

HAPTER 3. ACTIVITY 4: FACTS AND INFERENCES

URPOSES:

1. To distinguish between facts and inferences.
2. To rewrite inferences in a factual statement.

ISTRUCTIONS:

ead the inferences below. Rewrite them to be factual statements. If you don't know the "facts," indicate hat data you would need.

1. The U.S. is a violent and militaristic society.

____

2. Relationships on the Internet are better than face-to-face.

____

3. Everyone wants to be a U.S. citizen.

____

4. We would be more productive if everyone spoke at least two languages.

____

5. College students are lazy and unproductive.

____

eplace the opinions with factual statements that can be verified.

1. This is a better school than UM.

   Tuition is $100 lower and the student/teacher ratio is 20% lower here than at UM.

2. Europe is a better place to live than the U.S.

____

3. Communication courses are more valuable than physics.

____

4. People in the U.S. have lousy marriages.

____

5. Korean food is better than Chinese food.

____

NOTES ON LANGUAGE

NAME ______________________

HAPTER 3. ACTIVITY 5: EXPLORING THE WEB

IACHINE TRANSLATION

n order to "test" the power of machine translation, go to *http://babelfish.altavista.digital.com/egi-in/translate?*

1. Write out a simple command in English. (Go to the store and buy some eggs. Pick up my laundry on the way home. Put the book on the desk.)Write it here:

 ____

 Now, use the Web translator to translate from English into French, German, Portuguese, or Italian. (Use the "translate from" button.) If you are fluent in one of those languages, see how the Web's translation compares to yours. Once you have the translation, copy it and translate from that language back to English.

 ____

 ____

2. If the translation comes back differently (and even humorously) from your original English, speculate on what the difficulties were. It usually will not be exactly the same as your original; if it is exact, speculate why it would be.

 ____

 ____

3. Now try it with a more complex thought: your political ideas, your feelings about a complex issue. Go through the same steps as above:

 Sentence typed in: ______________________

 English re-translated: ______________________

4. What would you predict will happen? Why?

 ____

 ____

5. What properties of language account for some of the difficulties?

 ____

 ____

6. How would you assess the overall usefulness of a site like this to translate the home page of your university?

 ____

 ____

Just for fun, learn a bit about hieroglyphics and translate your name into hieroglyphics: *wysiwyg://141/http://www.quizland.com/hiero.pht*

Further exploration: Using a search engine, find a site that will translate your name into Japanese, Chinese, Arabic, or another language that does not use the alphabet English uses.

Web sites ______________________________

____

Speculate about what might happen if government officials relied on machine translation. ______________________________

____

____

NAME ______________________________

HAPTER 3 SELF TEST

ATCHING I (KEY TERMS)

atch each term listed on the left with its correct definition from the column on the right.

______ **1.** emotive language
______ **2.** connotation
______ **3.** behavioral description
______ **4.** factual statement
______ **5.** abstraction ladder
______ **6.** convergence
______ **7.** equivocation
______ **8.** high-context culture
______ **9.** equivocal words
______ **10.** jargon
______ **11.** divergence
______ **12.** euphemism
______ **13.** abstract language
______ **14.** low-context culture
______ **15.** denotation
______ **16.** slang

a. language that is not specific or detailed
b. a range of more-to-less abstract terms describing an event or object
c. an account that refers only to observable phenomena
d. the emotional associations of a term
e. linguistic strategy in which speakers emphasize their commonality with others through use of a similar language style
f. the objective, emotion-free definition of a term
g. words used by a particular group to differentiate itself, possibly by geographical region or age
h. words that convey the sender's attitude rather than objective description
i. words with more than one dictionary definition
j. vague statement that can be interpreted more than one way
k. pleasant-sounding term used in place of a less-pleasant one
l. statement that can be verified as true or false
m. culture which avoids direct use of language; meaning is conveyed through context more than words
n. a linguistic strategy in which speakers emphasize differences between their style and others to create distance
o. language shared by professionals or others with a common interest, such as medical shorthand, computer terms, or banking phrases
p. culture that relies heavily on language to make message explicit

MATCHING II

_______ **17.** inferential statement

_______ **18.** opinion statement

_______ **19.** Whorf–Sapir hypothesis

_______ **20.** phonological rules

_______ **21.** linguistic relativism

_______ **22.** relative words

_______ **23.** semantic rules

_______ **24.** sex role

_______ **25.** linguistic determinism

_______ **26.** pragmatic rules

_______ **27.** syntactic rules

_______ **28.** language

a. conclusion arrived at through interpretation of evidence
b. symbols, governed by rules, used to convey messages between persons
c. theory that a culture's world view is shaped and reflected by its language
d. moderate form of linguistic theory which argues that language strongly influences (but doesn't totally shape) people's perceptions
e. statement based on the speaker's beliefs
f. linguistic rules governing how sounds are combined to form words
g. rules that govern everyday use of language
h. rules that govern the meaning of words
i. words that gain their meaning by comparison
j. social orientation that governs behavior
k. rules that govern ways symbols are arranged
l. theory that the language used shapes the world view of its users

MULTIPLE CHOICE

Choose the BEST response from those listed.

1. If a person says "Book me to give the" instead of "Give the book to me," which kind of rule has most obviously been broken?

a. phonological
b. semantic
c. syntactic
d. pragmatic
e. none of the above

2. Language

a. is symbolic.
b. is rule-governed.
c. can shape attitudes.
d. can reflect attitudes.
e. all of the above

3. Using the same kind of language and language style as someone else can be a way to demonstrate _________ through convergence.

a. power
b. responsibility
c. affiliation
d. high-context
e. divergence

4. The statements "You make me disgusted" or "You make me happy" demonstrate a lack of ________.

a. convergence
b. status
c. credibility
d. semantics
e. responsibility

5. A boss hands a stack of papers to an assistant and tells him to "run these through the machine." He meant the copier; the assistant used the shredder. This is an example of ________ language.

a. jargon
b. pragmatic
c. equivocal
d. non–rule-governed
e. denotative

6. Saying "My husband had a vasectomy" or saying "My husband's been fixed" carries the same idea or denotation. The difference is that the words have very different ________.

a. behavioral descriptions
b. levels of abstraction
c. inferences
d. connotations
e. content

7. The fact that teachers gave different grades to the same papers when they were told the papers were written by students with various names seems to indicate the power of names to

a. create disruptions.
b. shape attitudes.
c. reflect attitudes.
d. avoid misunderstandings.
e. demonstrate linguistic relativism.

8. When persons decide whether to call themselves Mexican-American, Hispanic, Latino/a, or Chicano/a and others decide among Negro, Black, and African-American and still others decide among Euroamerican, Anglo, and white, the conscious choice of a name is a way in which persons use ________ to both shape and reflect attitudes toward themselves.

a. syntactic rules
b. equivocation
c. language
d. stereotypes
e. jargon

9. Which is true of men's speech, according to research cited in the text?

a. used to accomplish tasks more than to build intimate relationships
b. used often to disclose vulnerabilities
c. used to diminish status differences
d. rarely used to exert control
e. all of the above

10. Communicators in a high-context culture are more likely to

a. state feelings explicitly.
b. use language to build harmony.
c. ask for things they need directly.
d. engage in confrontation.
e. speak out about their needs.

11. After listening to a political speech, two listeners share their perceptions. One says, "He just beat around the bush and never got to the point." The second says, "He was quite interesting." It is probable that the first speaker

a. is from a low-context culture.
b. is from a high-context culture.
c. disproved the Whorf–Sapir hypothesis.
d. both a and c
e. none of the above

12. It is popular to use a variety of chilis for cooking. According to a recent *Newsweek* article, some of the most popular chilis have names like *prik khi nu,* which translates from Thai as "rat-dropping chili," and *chile tecpin*, which means "flea chili." When stores and markets use the chic-sounding foreign name rather than a less-pleasant translation, the foreign term acts as

a. a relative word.
b. an inference.
c. a behavioral description.
d. a succinct-style expression.
e. a euphemism.

13. Following Yitzhak Rabin's assassination, the Washington Bullets (whose team owner was Rabin's friend) announced that they would change their name because of the negative associations of the term "bullet." This change appears to be related to the ________ of the word.

a. denotations
b. connotations
c. inferences
d. equivocation
e. sequential placement

14. "Misunderstanding results when one person assumes that words mean the same thing to him or he as to all other persons." This is a paraphrase of which concept of language?

a. Many words have similar meanings.
b. Dictionaries are adequate for everyday language.
c. Meanings are in people, not in words.
d. Gender influences our language style and content.
e. Cultures have a preference for direct or indirect styles.

15. Which statement is least abstract (low-level abstraction)?

a. You're the best friend I've ever had.
b. I think you've just been terrific.
c. I appreciated your taking my son to the hospital.
d. You are so thoughtful.
e. I appreciate your friendship.

6. "I don't want to interrupt, but if we could start the meeting now . . ."

This is an example of
a. sequential placement.
b. tag question.
c. a disclaimer.
d. stereotyping.
e. perception check.

7. When you are unsure about what a person means by a statement, you could improve your understanding by using

a. a relative term.
b. a perception check.
c. an inference.
d. a syntactic rule.
e. terms that are more abstract than the other person used.

8. Which of the following is a problem with accepting dictionary definitions?

a. Many words have multiple definitions.
b. People often use words in ways you'd never be able to look up.
c. Dictionaries define most words in terms of other words.
d. All of the above are problems.
e. The dictionary definition is the best way to go and has no problems with meanings.

ATCHING III

_____ **1.** ambiguous language that has two or more equally plausible meanings

_____ **2.** cultures that avoid direct use of language, relying more on nonverbal messages and context

_____ **3.** an account that refers only to persons, contexts, and behaviors

_____ **4.** cultures that use language abundantly and rely on words for explanation and clarity

_____ **5.** beliefs about something that are not necessarily verifiable

a. behavioral description
b. equivocal
c. high-context cultures
d. low-context cultures
e. opinions

Match each situation with the type of language problem demonstrated.

_______ **6.** After promising not to raise taxes, the administration requires that additional money be paid by each person buying gasoline. It insists that this is not a new tax, but a "revenue enhancer."

_______ **7.** John promised to return your tape "soon" and you are angry because it is the end of the day and he has not returned it. John used *soon* to mean by the end of the week.

_______ **8.** I refer to my roommate as "arrogant and rude." After meeting her, you tell me that you thought she was "spirited and self-confident." Each of us has chosen _________.

_______ **9.** She didn't call on me when I raised my hand so she must not like me.

_______ **10.** A teen comes home from high school and says, "I wish I could get as high as Doug does each day." The mother is nervous because she thinks her child is referring to drugs; in fact, the teen is referring to the high jump in track.

a. emotive language
b. relative word
c. equivocal word
d. inference
e. euphemism

TRUE/FALSE

Circle the T or F to indicate whether you believe the statement is true or false. If it is **true,** give a **reas**[on] or an **example.** If it is **false, explain** what would make it true.

√ T F **1.** Our use of language rarely affects our credibility.

____

____

T F **2.** Phonological rules are those that govern the way sounds combine to form words.

____

____

√ T F **3.** Tag questions, intensifiers, and hedges are all types of powerful speech.

____

____

√ T F **4.** Women's speech tends to differ in content but not in goals from men's speech.

____

____

F **5.** Stereotyping and confusing others are frequent results of overly abstract speech.

____

____

OMPLETION

ll in each of the blanks with a phrase from the list provided. Choose the BEST word for each sentence. here are more words than you will use, but each word will be used only once.

gotiate meanings	**accomplish tasks**	**influence perception**
op thinking	**create misunderstanding**	**nourish relationships**

1. Men tend to use speech in order to ______________________.

2. The idea that the language which members of a culture speak can ______________________ is called the Whorf–Sapir hypothesis.

3. Women tend to use speech in order to ______________________.

4. In order to have effective communication when statements are ambiguous, it is necessary to ______________________.

5. Emotive and evasive language have the potential to ______________________.

CHAPTER 3 ANSWERS TO SELF TEST

MATCHING I (KEY TERMS)

1. h	**2.** d	**3.** c	**4.** l	**5.** b
6. e	**7.** j	**8.** m	**9.** i	**10.** o
11. n	**12.** k	**13.** a	**14.** p	**15.** f
16. g				

MATCHING II

17. a	**18.** e	**19.** c	**20.** f	**21.** d
22. i	**23.** h	**24.** j	**25.** l	**26.** g
27. k	**28.** b			

MULTIPLE CHOICE

1. c	**2.** e	**3.** c	**4.** e	**5.** c
6. d	**7.** b	**8.** c	**9.** a	**10.** b
11. a	**12.** e	**13.** b	**14.** c	**15.** c
16. c	**17.** b	**18.** d		

MATCHING III

1. b	**2.** c	**3.** a	**4.** d	**5.** e
6. e	**7.** b	**8.** a	**9.** d	**10.** c

TRUE/FALSE

1. F	**2.** T	**3.** F	**4.** F	**5.** T

COMPLETION

1. accomplish tasks
2. influence perception
3. nourish relationships
4. negotiate meanings
5. create misunderstanding

RELATED READING

"Antioch College Sexual Offense Policy, 1992."
Request a copy from Antioch College, 795 Livermore Street, Yellow Springs, OH 45387.

PREVIEW:

A "menace to spontaneous sex"? Or something that enables students to feel "more respected and more empowered"? The former is *Newsweek*'s description of the media's reaction to the Antioch (Ohio) College Sexual Offense Policy, 1992. The latter is one co-ed's reaction. The policy was instituted as a way of addressing the delicate issue of appropriate sexual conduct and concerns particularly about acquaintance rape. Read the policy in order to understand how it illustrates an attempt to induce the use of language—low-level abstractions and highly specific language—to grapple with issues of sexual conduct. The cornerstone of the policy is the need for "verbal consent at each new level of physical and/or sexual contact." As you read, look for ways in which the policy mandates the use of verbal language as well as ways the perceived need for the policy reflects principles in this chapter regarding the meaning of language, the power of language, and the language of misunderstandings.

REVIEW:

1. How does the policy reflect a belief in the power of language? What principles of language are reflected in this policy?
2. Do you think encouraging people to use more low-level abstractions more often while discussing their sexual desires will reduce acquaintance rape? Will following the policy make words less equivocal?
3. Would someone from a low-context or high-context culture be more comfortable with this policy? Why?
4. Would there be difficulty enforcing/living up to the policy even for those in a traditionally low-context culture like the U.S.? Why or why not?
5. What is your reaction to the line, "If someone has initially consented but then stops consenting during a sexual interaction, she/he should communicate withdrawal verbally and/or through physical resistance."

NOTES ON LANGUAGE

Chapter 4
Listening

AFTER STUDYING THIS CHAPTER, YOU WILL BETTER UNDERSTAND:

1. The most common misconceptions about listening.
2. The five components of the listening process.
3. The most common types of ineffective listening.
4. The challenges that make effective listening difficult.
5. The skills necessary to listen effectively in informational, critical, and empathic settings.

AFTER STUDYING THIS CHAPTER, YOU WILL BE BETTER ABLE TO:

1. Identify situations where you listen ineffectively and explain the reasons for your lack of effectiveness.
2. Identify the consequences of your ineffective listening.
3. Follow the guidelines for informational listening.
4. Analyze an argument or claim by evaluating the credibility of its proponent, the quality of evidence offered, and the soundness of its reasoning.
5. In an empathic listening context, apply appropriate response styles.

CHAPTER 4 SKELETON OUTLINE

This outline can be a helpful study tool to assist you in seeing the order and sequence of the chapter and the relationship of ideas. Use it to take notes as you read and/or to add concepts presented in lecture.

I. **MISCONCEPTIONS ABOUT LISTENING**
   - A. Listening and hearing are different.
     1. Hearing
     2. Listening
        - a. attending
        - b. understanding
        - c. responding
        - d. remembering
          - (1) rate of forgetting
          - (2) residual message
   - B. Listening is not natural.
   - C. Listening requires effort.
   - D. Listeners receive different messages.

II. **OVERCOMING CHALLENGES TO EFFECTIVE LISTENING**
   - A. Faulty listening behaviors
     1. Pseudolistening
     2. Selective listening
     3. Defensive listening
     4. Ambushing

5. Insulated listening
6. Insensitive listening
7. Stage hogging

B. Reasons for poor listening
1. Effort
2. Message overload
3. Rapid thought
4. Psychological noise
5. Physical noise
6. Hearing problems
7. Faulty assumptions
8. Talking's apparent advantages
9. Media influences

III. INFORMATIONAL LISTENING

A. Don't argue or judge prematurely.

B. Separate message and speaker.

C. Be opportunistic.

D. Look for key ideas.

E. Ask questions.
1. Sincere questions
2. Counterfeit questions
   a. questions that make statements
   b. questions that carry hidden agendas
   c. questions that seek "correct" answers
   d. questions based on unchecked assumptions

F. Paraphrase.
1. Define
2. Advantages
   a. more accurate understanding
   b. sincere understanding
3. Methods
   a. change wording
   b. offer an example
   c. reflect underlying theme

G. Take notes.
1. Don't wait too long before taking notes.
2. Record any key ideas.
3. Develop a note-taking format.

IV. CRITICAL LISTENING (EVALUATIVE LISTENING)

A. Listen for information before evaluating.

B. Evaluate the speaker's credibility.
1. Competence
2. Impartiality

C. Examine the speaker's evidence.

D. Examine emotional appeals.
1. Recent evidence
2. Enough evidence
3. Source of evidence
4. Interpretation of evidence

E. Examine the speaker's reasoning for fallacies.

V. EMPATHIC LISTENING

A. Advising
1. Requests not always clear

2. Advice not always best, others avoid responsibility
   a. Is it the correct advice?
   b. Will other accept it?
   c. Will you be blamed?

B. Judging
   1. Did person request your judgment?
   2. Is your judgment constructive?

C. Analyzing
   1. Be tentative.
   2. Be reasonably correct.
   3. Be sure the other is receptive.
   4. Be well-motivated.

D. Questioning
   1. Don't ask for curiosity.
   2. Be sure questions are not confusing or distracting.
   3. Don't disguise suggestions or criticism as questions.

E. Supporting
   1. Be sure you're sincere.
   2. Be sure other can accept your support.

F. Prompting

G. Paraphrasing
   1. Helps speaker clarify problem
   2. Helps listener understand thoughts and feelings
      a. problem's complexity
      b. adequate time and concern
      c. genuine interest
      d. withhold judgment
      e. proportion to other responses

H. When and how to help?
   1. Situation
   2. Other person
   3. Yourself

HAPTER 4 KEY TERMS

his list of key terms corresponds to those in boldface in your text. Use these lines to write the efinition and/or an example of the word on the line next to it.

lvising ____

____

nbushing ____

____

nalyzing ____

____

ttending ____

____

itical listening ____

____

defensive listening ____________________

____

empathic listening ____________________

____

hearing ____________________

____

informational listening ____________________

____

insensitive listening ____________________

____

insulated listening ____________________

____

judging response ____________________

____

listening ____________________

____

paraphrasing ____________________

____

pseudolistening ____________________

____

questioning ____________________

____

residual message ____________________

____

selective listening ____________________

____

stage hogging ____________________

____

supporting ____________________

____

NAME ______________________________

HAPTER 4. ACTIVITY 1: AN ANALYSIS OF POOR LISTENING

JRPOSES:

1. To analyze poor listening.
2. To identify ways to improve listening.

ISTRUCTIONS:

1. Choose one situation in which you listened poorly.
2. Fill in the following chart to carefully analyze each factor that affected your listening.

N EXAMPLE OF POOR LISTENING

ntext:

riefly describe where you were, who else was there, what was happening, and why it was important to sten well, even though you didn't.

____

____

a listener:

was not attending (paying attention to) the message because of interference of the following factors.

escribe your particular **needs** and how they adversely affected your listening. ______________

____

escribe your particular **wants/desires** and how they adversely affected your listening. ______________

____

escribe your particular **interests** and how they adversely affected your listening. ______________

____

escribe your particular **attitudes** and how they adversely affected your listening. ______________

____

escribe your particular **goals** and how they adversely affected your listening. ______________

____

escribe your particular **past experiences** and how they adversely affected your listening. ______________

____

escribe your particular **habits** and how they adversely affected your listening. ______________

____

I was selectively listening for ____________________ and that affected my listening adversely because I was not understanding the

_______ syntax

_______ semantics

_______ pragmatics

_______ effort exerted

_______ motivation

_______ intelligence

_______ message itself was clear to me

_______ channel was familiar to me

My own responses were less than desirable because I: (check those that apply)

_______ lacked eye contact

_______ failed to lean forward

_______ didn't stop other activities to listen

_______ didn't turn toward speaker/turned away from speaker

_______ had a facial expression that was inappropriate

_______ failed to use paraphrasing

_______ asked irrelevant or threatening questions

Other problems were that

_______ I was experiencing message overload because ____________________________________

_______ I used my spare time unwisely by ____________________________________

_______ There was too much psychological noise because ____________________________________

_______ There was too much physical noise such as ____________________________________

_______ I have a hearing problem which made this difficult ____________________________________

I bought into some of these faulty assumptions while listening

_______ I assumed I'd heard this all before because ____________________________________

_______ I assumed the speaker was too simple because ____________________________________

_______ I assumed the speaker was too complex because ____________________________________

_______ I assumed the speaker was unimportant because ____________________________________

Summary:

What have you learned from this analysis that may help you prevent these listening problems in the future? If you were to give yourself one piece of advice, what would it be?

____

____

____

____

____

NAME ______________________________

[CH]APTER 4. ACTIVITY 2: AN ANALYSIS OF GOOD LISTENING

[PU]RPOSES:

- To analyze good listening.
- To identify strengths in listening.

[IN]STRUCTIONS:

- Choose one situation in which you listened well.
- Fill in the following charts to analyze each area and tell how or why each factor affected your listening in a positive way.

[SI]TUATION

[Bri]efly describe where you were, who else was there, and what was happening.

____

____

[As] a listener:

[I w]as attending (paying attention to) the message because of the following factors.

[De]scribe your particular **needs** and how they positively affected your listening. ______________

____

[De]scribe your particular **wants/desires** and how they positively affected your listening. ______________

____

[De]scribe your particular **interests** and how they positively affected your listening. ______________

____

[De]scribe your particular **attitudes** and how they positively affected your listening. ______________

____

[De]scribe your particular **goals** and how they positively affected your listening. ______________

____

[De]scribe your particular **past experiences** and how they positively affected your listening. ______________

____

[De]scribe your particular **habits** and how they positively affected your listening. ______________

____

[I w]as selectively listening for ____________________ and that affected my listening positively. I was [un]derstanding the

_____ syntax

_____ semantics

_______ pragmatics

_______ Effort was exerted.

_______ There was motivation to listen.

_______ The message itself was clear to me.

_______ The channel was familiar to me.

My own responses involved: (check those that apply)

_______ eye contact

_______ forward lean

_______ stopping other activities to listen

_______ turning toward speaker

_______ using a facial expression that was appropriate

_______ paraphrasing

_______ asking nonthreatening questions

I avoided message overload by ____

____

I used my spare time wisely by ____

____

I minimized psychological noise by ____________________________________

____

I minimized physical noise such as ____________________________________

by ____

I ______ do ______ do not have a hearing problem which made this difficult.

I avoided these faulty assumptions while listening.

_______ Instead of thinking, "I've heard this all before," I was thinking ____________

____

_______ Instead of thinking, "The speaker is too simple," I was thinking ____________

____

_______ Instead of thinking, "The speaker is too complex," I was thinking ____________

____

_______ Instead of thinking, "The speaker is unimportant," I was thinking ____________

____

NAME ______________________________

IAPTER 4. ACTIVITY 3: PARAPHRASING

RPOSE:

. To practice paraphrasing and observe the process of paraphrasing.

STRUCTIONS:

. Choose two people to work with. Designate yourselves "A," "B," and "C."
. "A" should choose one of the following quotations to discuss, preferably one which you feel strongly about. After reading the quotation, "A" begins by commenting and giving his/her opinions and feelings about it. [At this time "C" is observing both "A" and "B" and filling out Part B.]
. "B" now paraphrases what "A" said to "A"'s satisfaction before adding to the discussion. Then "B" expresses a feeling/opinion on it and "A" paraphrases before adding to the discussion. Except for "A"'s first comment, no one speaks until the other person has paraphrased to the satisfaction of the person who made the comment.
. After about five minutes of discussion, "C" reports his/her observations on the listening skills of "A" and "B."
. Repeat the steps above with "B" starting a conversation, "C" listening and responding, and "A" observing. Then repeat the steps above with "C" starting a conversation, "A" listening and responding, and "B" observing.
. When you have finished three rounds (two as listener/one as observer), fill out Part C individually. After you've finished, share your responses with each other.

tations to choose from:

e unused coat in your closet **belongs** to the man who needs it. —St. Basil

m what we get, we can make a living; what we give, however, makes a life. —Arthur Ashe

ppiness is having a large, loving, caring, close-knit family in another city. —George Burns

ve does not consist in gazing at each other, but in looking outward together in the same direction. ntoine de Saint-Exupery

ere are two tragedies in life: not getting what you want and getting what you want.

netimes it's a little better to travel than to arrive. —Robert Pirsig *(Zen and the Art of Motorcycle intenance)*

ucation is the ability to listen to almost anything without losing your temper or your Self-confidence. obert Frost

ere's a fine line between being on the leading edge and being in the lunatic fringe. —Frank Armstrong *eparing for Tomorrow's Challenges)*

ucation is not filling a bucket but lighting a fire. —William Butler Yeats

e first person will give his or her reaction to the quotation you've chosen. From then on, speak only er paraphrasing the other to his/her satisfaction.

PART B. OBSERVER FORM

As you observe both persons, try to comment on each of these factors:

Person A's name ____

Did it appear that ______ effort was exerted? ______ there was motivation to listen?

Was there appropriate (check those that apply)

_______ eye contact

_______ forward lean

_______ lack of distracting behaviors (pencil tapping, foot tapping)

_______ body orientation (turned toward speaker)

_______ facial expression

_______ paraphrasing of facts

_______ paraphrasing of feelings

_______ asking nonthreatening questions

What would you say are this person's strengths as a listener?

____

____

____

____

____

____

____

If you could make one comment on something for this listener to improve on, what would it be?

____

____

____

____

____

____

____

erson B's name ____

id it appear that ______ effort was exerted? ______ there was motivation to listen?

'as there appropriate (check those that apply)

______ eye contact

______ forward lean

______ lack of distracting behaviors (pencil tapping, foot tapping)

______ body orientation (turned toward speaker)

______ facial expression

______ paraphrasing of facts

______ paraphrasing of feelings

______ asking nonthreatening questions

'hat would you say are this person's strengths as a listener?

____

____

____

____

____

____

____

you could make one comment on something for this listener to improve on, what would it be?

____

____

____

____

____

____

____

PART C

After your conversation, fill in the following:

1. What was your **initial** reaction to the exercise?

2. What nonverbal behaviors did you observe in yourself and your partner initially?

3. Did these change as time went on? How?

4. Describe the **effect** paraphrasing had on your conversation?

5. How did it differ from other, more typical conversations? If you hadn't been trying to paraphrase, predict the direction and tone of the conversation that might have ensued.

6. What are some phrases you and your partner used to paraphrase?

7. How did you **feel** when your partner tried to paraphrase your answers and tried to understand what you were saying?

____

____

8. Were there any ways that your self-concept or your own perception influenced how you understood or misunderstood what your partner was saying? Explain.

____

____

____

____

9. How would you sum up what you learned from this exercise?

____

____

____

____

NOTES ON LISTENING

NAME ____________________

ARIATION OF CHAPTER 4. ACTIVITY 3: PARAPHRASING

STENING ABOUT LISTENING

l:

e goal of this assignment is to provide you an opportunity to practice and sharpen listening and raphrasing skills. The goal of this assignment is **not** self-disclosure or friendship, but rather a clearer derstanding of the **process** and requirements of listening actively.

ting:

range to carry out the dyad interview in a place that is comfortable for you—cafeteria, outdoor tables. cus on the interview and try to tune out distractions.

ne:

–75 minutes.

cedure:

. Statements should be completed in the order in which they appear.
. You may decline to answer any question; just say "pass."
. Treat information with respect and confidentiality; **take no notes,** listen and paraphrase for better understanding.

ening.

st, one person completes statement one; then the second person completes the same statement. Do e same for statements 2–4. Alternate speaking and listening roles throughout the exercise

. One thing I like or dislike about my name is . . .
. When I got this listening assignment I thought . . .
. When we got this listening assignment I felt . . .
. When I hear the word "listen" I think . . .

dy.

om here on, one person will **complete** a statement and **expand** on it. The other person will listen and en **paraphrase.** Use your **own different words** to paraphrase what you think the other person is ying, both **thoughts and feelings.** The other person must verify that that is what he/she means or arify it so the "listener" can correctly paraphrase. The "listener" must correctly paraphrase to the tisfaction of the "speaker." **Switch roles** so each person completes and expands on the same statement fore going on to the next.

. The best role model of listening I've ever known/seen is/was . . . because . . .
. If you ask my friends, they'd say that in terms of listening I . . .
. When someone is really listening to me, I know he/she is listening because . . .
. When someone really listens to me I feel . . .
. When someone isn't listening to me I feel . . .
. When someone isn't really listening to me, I know he/she isn't listening because . . .
. I find it very difficult to listen when . . .
. I find it very difficult to listen to . . .
. I find it easy to listen when . . .
. I find it easy to listen to . . .

Break.

Now stop and talk about how you're doing. Then practice paraphrasing some more.

15. If parents really listened to children, I think the impact on families would be that . . .
16. If world leaders listened to each other, I think the world would . . .
17. If bosses really listened to employees, I would predict that . . .
18. If politicians really listened to constituents, I would predict that . . .
19. For me, the hardest thing (barrier) about listening to significant others is that . . .
20. I do/don't think that listening is related to academic success because . . .
Do you believe that students who get better grades are smarter or listen better?
Do you believe that student success is dependent on listening ability or motivation?
21. Listening courses should/should not be required in school because . . .
22. Listening courses should/should not be required of college instructors because . . .
23. In order to graduate, students should [not] demonstrate listening skills by . . .
24. Much of what I know and believe about listening I learned from . . .

Conclusion.

25. When I think of how we've completed this exercise I think/feel . . .

What I've learned about listening . . .

NAME ______________________________

APTER 4. ACTIVITY 4: LISTENING STYLES

RPOSES:

. To identify various listening styles.
. To evaluate the advantages and disadvantages of each style in particular contexts.

STRUCTIONS:

. Read each of the following scenarios.
. Construct a response that represents each of the styles of listening.
. Consider the consequences of each style by responding to the questions.

. Your best friend is telling you about his/her concerns about the person he/she has been seeing for two years. They had always planned to marry after college, but now your friend says, "I'm just feeling like we never really dated anyone else seriously. I love Pat, but I wonder if we should see other people while we're still in college. I don't think we'll know if we're right for each other if we don't really know anyone else."

advising response ______________________________

____

judging response ______________________________

____

analyzing response ______________________________

____

questioning response ______________________________

____

supporting response ______________________________

____

prompting response ______________________________

____

paraphrasing response ______________________________

____

Which response(s) do you think would be likely to harm the relationship? Why?

____

____

Which response do you think would be best? Why? ______________________________

____

____

2. Two friends have been advised by their physician that they fit the profile of someone at higher tha average risk for Hepatitis B. Their health plan won't pay for the vaccines (about $250). They are considering getting the vaccine, but are concerned about the cost. One says to you, "I know I'm ir high-risk group, but I'm not sure there's much chance of getting it. I haven't really known anyone who has. What would you do?"

advising response ______________________________

____

judging response ______________________________

____

analyzing response ______________________________

____

questioning response ______________________________

____

supporting response ______________________________

____

prompting response ______________________________

____

paraphrasing response ______________________________

____

Which response(s) do you think would be likely to harm the relationship? Why?

____

____

Which response do you think would be best? Why? ______________________________

____

____

3. Your supervisor is considering allowing some employees (including you) to begin to experiment with flexible hours. She is discussing the idea with you and a few other employees before work one morning. She says, "I'd really like to have some of you try flex hours and see the impact on morale and productivity. I know some of you have concerns about transportation and child care, and others are trying to take classes and work. But if some are allowed to try flex hours and all aren't, i could create more hard feelings. I can't make it department wide without my district manager's okay, and he's not willing to try it. But I do have leeway to experiment on a small scale. I wonder what would be best."

advising response ______________________________

____

judging response ______________________________

____

analyzing response ______________________________

____

questioning response ______________________________

____

supporting response ______________________________

____

prompting response ______________________________

____

paraphrasing response ______________________________

____

Which response(s) do you think would be likely to harm the relationship? Why?

____

____

Which response do you think would be best? Why? ______________________________

____

____

A co-worker with whom you must coordinate projects says, "Ever since my brother was killed in that car accident, I just haven't felt like this job is important. I haven't felt that much of anything is important. I can't focus or concentrate very well, and nothing matters much. I'm sorry I've caused you to miss some deadlines, too."

advising response ______________________________

____

judging response ______________________________

____

analyzing response ______________________________

____

questioning response ______________________________

____

supporting response ______________________________

____

prompting response ______________________________

____

paraphrasing response ______________________________

____

Which response(s) do you think would be likely to harm the relationship? Why?

____

____

Which response do you think would be best? Why? ______________________________

____

____

NAME ____________________

HAPTER 4. ACTIVITY 5: EXPLORING THE WEB

STENING COMPETENCIES

e National Communication Association has outlined a set of listening competencies, or behaviors and tening skills that are expected of students. Look at *http://www.natcom.org/instrresour/ llege_competencies_table1.htm* to see the set of listening competencies needed for literal mprehension and critical comprehension.

Compare and contrast the definition of listening given in your text with the definition in the ragraph at the beginning of the Listening Competencies.

. What are the four competencies listed under being able to listen with literal comprehension (A, B, C, D)?

. Do you think there are others that should be listed? Explain.

. List the competencies associated with being able to listen with critical comprehension (A through J).

. In your own words, what does competency J-1 mean?

. What term used in your book for a type of listening parallels the term "literal comprehension" as used in these competencies?

6. What term parallels "critical comprehension"?

7. Compare and contrast the competencies shown for literal and for critical comprehension.

8. How would you explain the fact that there are ten competencies under critical listening compared to four under literal comprehension?

9. Now, look at the standards (numbers 13–15) for competent listeners in grades K–12 as defined by NCA. These are illustrated in chart form with separate categories of knowledge, behaviors, and attitudes and can be found at *http://www.natcom.org/instrresour/ Standards_and_Competencies 1998/S&C_13-15.htm.* Choose two of the knowledge items in Standard 13 (Numbers 13-1 through 13-19). Can you "answer" the questions? Are there any you cannot respond to with accurate knowledge? Which ones?

10. Do you think it is realistic for high school students to be able to have and demonstrate this knowledge? Why or why not?

11. What is standard 15?

12. List the barriers presented in items 15-2 through 15-12. Which of those barriers correspond directly to barriers in your text? Are there any listed in your text and not here? Any listed in this Web site and not in your text? Are there any barriers you can think of that are not listed in either place and should be? Fill in the chart to answer.

LIST BARRIERS 15-2 THROUGH 15-12	LIST SIMILAR BARRIER NAMED IN TEXT	CHECK HERE IF NOT LISTED IN TEXT	LIST ANY ADDITIONAL BARRIERS NOT FOUND EITHER PLACE

13. Overall, how valuable do you think these competencies would be for elementary teachers to use in evaluating their students?

___

___

___

___

NOTES ON LISTENING

NAME ____________________

CHAPTER 4 SELF TEST

MATCHING (KEY TERMS)

Match each term listed on the left with its correct definition from the column on the right. Choose the most specific definition.

_______ **1.** defensive listening
_______ **2.** supporting
_______ **3.** questioning
_______ **4.** paraphrasing
_______ **5.** advising
_______ **6.** analyzing
_______ **7.** pseudolistening
_______ **8.** insulated listening
_______ **9.** ambushing
_______ **10.** stage hogging
_______ **11.** empathic listening
_______ **12.** selective listening
_______ **13.** informational listening
_______ **14.** critical listening
_______ **15.** attending
_______ **16.** hearing
_______ **17.** insensitive listening
_______ **18.** residual message
_______ **19.** listening
_______ **20.** judging response

a. the process wherein sound waves strike the eardrum and cause vibrations that are transmitted to the brain
b. the process of focusing on certain stimuli from the environment
c. listening in which the goal is to judge the quality or accuracy of the speaker's remarks
d. response style in which the receiver reassures, comforts, or distracts the person seeking help
e. a listening style in which the receiver is more concerned with making his or her own point than with understanding the speaker
f. the part of a message a receiver can recall after short- and long-term memory loss
g. a style of listening (helping) in which the receiver seeks additional information from the sender
h. an imitation of true listening in which the receiver pretends to listen but has his/her mind elsewhere
i. a helping style in which the listener offers an interpretation of a speaker's message
j. a listening style in which the receiver listens carefully to gather information to use in an attack on the speaker
k. feedback in which the receiver rewords the speaker's thoughts and feelings
l. listening in which the goal is to receive accurately the same thoughts the speaker is trying to convey
m. listening in which the goal is to help the speaker solve a problem
n. a reaction in which the receiver evaluates the sender's message either favorably or unfavorably
o. a listening style in which the receiver responds only to messages that interest him or her
p. a response style in which the receiver perceives a speaker's comments as an attack
q. failure to recognize the thoughts or feelings that are not directly expressed by a speaker, instead, accepting the speaker's words at face value
r. process wherein the brain reconstructs electrochemical impulses generated by hearing into representations of the original sound and gives them meaning
s. a helping response in which the receiver offers suggestions about how the speaker should deal with a problem
t. style in which the receiver ignores undesirable information

MULTIPLE CHOICE

Choose the BEST response from those listed.

1. Of these activities, which one occupies a greater percentage of most persons' day?

a. listening to face-to-face messages
b. listening to mass media
c. writing
d. speaking
e. reading

2. Research cited in your text shows listening to be a significant factor in

a. marital relationships.
b. family relationships.
c. career success.
d. persuasive skills.
e. all of the above.

3. The stages of listening include all BUT

a. attending.
b. understanding.
c. responding.
d. activating.
e. remembering.

4. Which is true?

a. Listening and hearing are remarkably similar.
b. Listening and hearing are exactly the same process.
c. Listening is physical; hearing is psychological.
d. It is possible to listen without hearing.
e. It is possible to hear without listening.

5. Which is true?

a. Listening is a natural process.
b. Listening requires effort.
c. All listeners receive the same message.
d. All of the above are true.
e. None of the above is true.

6. Nodding and smiling and pretending to listen is called ________.

a. selective listening
b. defensive listening
c. stage hogging
d. pseudolistening
e. insensitive listening

7. If we barely pay attention to another person's messages until she/he starts to talk about a co-worke and then we pay attention for the "dirt" on him/her, we are engaged in ________.

a. pseudolistening
b. insensitive listening
c. defensive listening
d. ambushing
e. critical listening

8. Generally people speak between 100 and 140 words a minute, but are capable of understanding speech at ________ words per minute.

a. 300
b. 250
c. 200
d. 150
e. 100

9. Listening is poor when

a. we don't expend the effort.
b. we experience message overload.
c. we experience psychological noise.
d. all of the above
e. none of the above

10. Which of these is a faulty assumption discussed in your text?

a. "I've heard this before."
b. "This is too hard to understand."
c. "This is too easy."
d. "This is boring and not very important."
e. All of these are faulty assumptions.

11. When listening for information, it is wise to

a. make some quick judgments about the speaker, so you're not misled.
b. tie the message and speaker together in your mind.
c. be opportunistic by learning what you can from this speaker, even if you learn what not to do.
d. listen for details rather than thesis.
e. all of the above

12. Which of these is a sincere question?

a. Can you help me understand why this is so difficult for you?
b. Why are you acting so weird?
c. Are you finally getting a promotion?
d. Do you still have a weight problem?
e. none of the above

13. Which is the best paraphrase of "I'm just in such a rut; I'm unhappy with work and with my relationship. Seems like everything's the same day after day after day."

a. Why don't you jazz up your life by doing something different?
b. Sounds like you don't feel much excitement and like you're maybe bored with the routine.
c. Seems like your problem is that you haven't put yourself in any new situations lately.
d. What are you unhappy with: not having a mate or not being promoted?
e. All are equally good paraphrases.

14. When would you use critical listening?

a. When your special friend is having a difficult time at work.
b. When you need to know what time a meeting is being held.
c. When you are the object of a sales pitch.
d. When a friend has lost a close election and is very upset.
e. All of these would be appropriate times for critical listening.

15. A fallacy is an error in ________.

a. listening
b. reasoning
c. speaking
d. advising
e. expressing

TRUE/FALSE

Circle the T or F to indicate whether you believe the statement is true or false. If it is **true**, give a **reaso** or an **example**. If it is **false**, **explain** what would make it true.

T F **1.** Examining emotional appeals is a part of empathic listening.

____

____

T F **2.** Analyzing may create defensiveness in another.

____

____

T F **3.** All questioning responses are confusing or distracting to a person with a problem.

____

____

T F **4.** Supporting responses are always perceived as reassuring and encouraging.

____

____

T F **5.** Paraphrasing involves paraphrasing both thoughts and feelings.

____

____

COMPLETION

Fill in each of the blanks with a word from the list provided. Choose the BEST word for each sentence There are more words than you will use, but each word will be used only once.

understanding	**listening**	**responding**	**remembering**
attending	**hearing**		

1. ________________ is a physiological process; listening is psychological.

2. ________________ to a message involves giving observable feedback to the speaker.

3. Individual needs, wants, and interests help determine whether you will be ____________________ to a message.

4. Making sense of a message is called ____________________ and requires understanding syntax and semantics.

5. The size of the residual message from any event has to do with the final step in the listening process, ____________________.

CHAPTER 4 ANSWERS TO SELF TEST

MATCHING (KEY TERMS)

1. p	**2.** d	**3.** g	**4.** k	**5.** s
6. i	**7.** h	**8.** t	**9.** j	**10.** e
11. m	**12.** o	**13.** l	**14.** c	**15.** b
16. a	**17.** q	**18.** f	**19.** r	**20.** n

MULTIPLE CHOICE

1. a	**2.** e	**3.** d	**4.** e	**5.** b
6. d	**7.** d	**8.** a	**9.** d	**10.** e
11. c	**12.** a	**13.** b	**14.** c	**15.** b

TRUE/FALSE

1. F	**2.** T	**3.** F	**4.** F	**5.** T

COMPLETION

1. hearing	**2.** responding	**3.** attending	**4.** understanding	**5.** remembering

ELATED READING

A Lesson in Listening," by Deanna Wylie Mayer, *Sojourners Magazine,* 24, no. 2 (May–June 1995): 37.

REVIEW:

arriers to authentic listening abound. Listening to one another on emotional topics is especially tough. his article advocates really listening, even when we may have an agenda or a desire to use someone se's story for our own purposes. Before reading this article, be up front with yourself about how your eliefs about abortion and women who have had abortions bias or present barriers for you when stening. What kind of speakers or writers are you ready and willing to listen to with an open mind? hich ones do you listen to defensively? Selectively? With insulation or ready to ambush? Can you set side your own biases and avoid arguing or judging prematurely? Before reading, prepare yourself to sten to really understand the writer and to empathetically listen to "Jeanne's story," a story within the ading.

EVIEW:

1. Before re-telling Jeanne's story, the author cautions us not to "use" her story to support or negate positions we advocate or denounce, but to just listen. As both sides, pro-choice and pro-life, listen to a story like this one, what kind of listening might they tend to use?
2. What kind of listening discussed in the text would be equivalent to what this author asks us to do, "just listening?"
3. What kind of listening does Jeanne imply that both pro-choice and pro-life groups have done in the past?
4. What other issues would you say are on a par with this one, in terms of being as emotional and as difficult for people to listen to each other?
5. Paraphrase the author's main point.

NOTES ON LISTENING

Chapter 5
Nonverbal Communication

FTER STUDYING THIS CHAPTER, YOU WILL BETTER UNDERSTAND:

1. Five characteristics of nonverbal communication.
2. Three differences between verbal and nonverbal communication.
3. Six functions nonverbal communication can serve.
4. How the types of nonverbal communication described in this chapter function.

FTER STUDYING THIS CHAPTER, YOU WILL BE BETTER ABLE TO:

1. Identify and describe the various nonverbal communication categories of yourself and others in various contexts.
2. Identify nonverbal behaviors that repeat, substitute for, complement, accent, regulate, and contradict verbal messages.
3. Recognize the emotional and relational dimensions of your own nonverbal behavior.
4. Share your interpretation of another person's nonverbal behavior in a tentative manner when such sharing is appropriate.

HAPTER 5 SKELETON OUTLINE

his outline can be a helpful study tool to assist you in seeing the order and sequence of the chapter and e relationship of ideas. Use it to take notes as you read and/or to add concepts presented in lecture.

I. **CHARACTERISTICS OF NONVERBAL COMMUNICATION**
   - A. Nonverbal communication exists.
   - B. Nonverbal behavior has communicative value.
     1. Unintentional
     2. Unconscious
   - C. Nonverbal communication is primarily relational.
     1. Identity management
     2. Define relationships
     3. Express attitudes and feelings
   - D. Nonverbal communication is ambiguous.
     1. Context
     2. History of relationship
     3. Other's mood
     4. Your feelings
   - E. Nonverbal communication is culture-bound..
     1. Gestures vary
     2. Distances
     3. Eye contact
     4. Intonation

II. DIFFERENCES BETWEEN VERBAL AND NONVERBAL

- **A.** Single vs. multiple channels
- **B.** Discrete vs. continuous
- **C.** Conscious vs. unconscious

III. FUNCTIONS OF NONVERBAL COMMUNICATION

- **A.** Repeating (emblems)
- **B.** Substituting
- **C.** Complementing (illustrators)
- **D.** Accenting
- **E.** Regulating
- **F.** Contradicting
  - **1.** Nonverbal carries more weight
  - **2.** Interpreting honesty
  - **3.** Detecting deception

IV. TYPES OF NONVERBAL COMMUNICATION

- **A.** Posture and gesture
  - **1.** Kinesics
  - **2.** Manipulators
- **B.** Face and eyes
  - **1.** Quantity and speed of expressions
  - **2.** Basic expressions and affect blends
- **C.** Voice (paralanguage)
  - **1.** Tone, speed, pitch, volume, pauses, disfluencies
  - **2.** Compliance, contradiction, perception
- **D.** Touch
  - **1.** Earliest contact
  - **2.** Need
  - **3.** Type of relationship
  - **4.** Type of touch
- **E.** Physical attractiveness
- **F.** Clothing
- **G.** Distance
  - **1.** Intimate
  - **2.** Personal
  - **3.** Social
  - **4.** Public
- **H.** Time (chronemics)
  - **1.** Status
  - **2.** Culture
- **I.** Territoriality
- **J.** Environment
  - **1.** Provides information (impression)
  - **2.** Shapes interaction

APTER 5 KEY TERMS

is list of key terms corresponds to those in boldface in your text. Use these lines to write the inition and/or an example of the word on the line next to it.

ct blend ______________________________

____

onemics ______________________________

____

fluency ______________________________

____

blems ______________________________

____

strators ______________________________

____

imate distance ______________________________

____

esics ______________________________

____

nipulators ______________________________

____

xed messages ______________________________

____

nverbal communication ______________________________

____

ralanguage ______________________________

____

rsonal distance ______________________________

____

oxemics ______________________________

____

public distance ____

____

social distance ____

____

territory ____

____

Sketch some emblems here:

Sketch some facial expressions here:

Bridgewater State College

JOHN JOSEPH MOAKLEY CENTER
FOR TECHNOLOGICAL APPLICATIONS
BRIDGEWATER STATE COLLEGE
BRIDGEWATER, MASSACHUSETTS 02325

P11 – Char. of Comp. Communicator

P43 – Impression Management wk

P67 – Skip ∅

P99 Listening wk

P125 NV wk

P157 – Self disclosure/Johari W. wk

P187 – Interp. wk

P221 – grp wk

P249 – grp collab – wk

279 – Topic Selection wk

309 –

333 (wk)

NAME ______________________________

HAPTER 5. ACTIVITY 1: CATEGORIES OF NONVERBAL BEHAVIOR

JRPOSE:

1. To analyze and categorize nonverbal behaviors.

ISTRUCTIONS:

1. Read the paragraph below.
2. Underline as many references as you can to different types of nonverbal communication.
3. Draw a line from the words to the margin and write the words describing the type of nonverbal behavior in the margin: posture and gesture, face and eyes, voice, touch, physical attractiveness, clothing, distance, time, territoriality, environment.

xample:

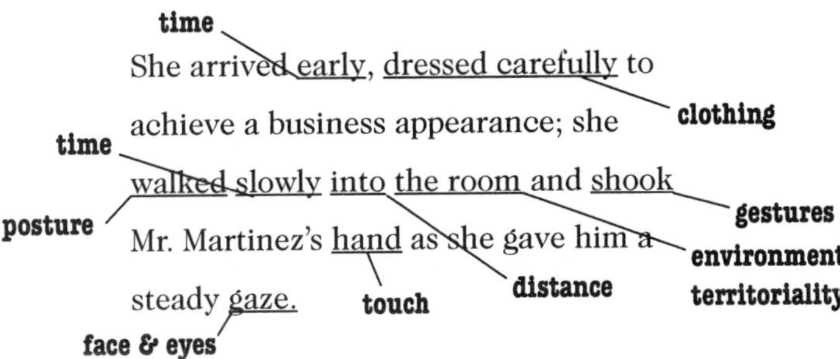

OUR TURN:

lip two or three paragraphs from a news article which makes many references to nonverbal ommunication. Tape the article in the space below. Underline and label each type of nonverbal ommunication referred to.

NOTES ON NONVERBAL COMMUNICATION

NAME ______________________________

APTER 5. ACTIVITY 2: NONVERBAL IMPRESSION MANAGEMENT

RPOSE:

To develop skills in using nonverbal communication to manage impressions and define relationships.

STRUCTIONS:

Read each situation. After reading it, describe as many nonverbal behaviors as you think are appropriate to help you manage the situation.

After recording your own thoughts, compare responses with your classmates.

Use as many **types** of nonverbal behavior as you deem appropriate: posture and gesture, face and eyes, voice, touch, physical attractiveness, clothing, distance, time, territoriality, environment.

RT 1. IDENTITY MANAGEMENT

You want to be seen as a competent and conscientious person who is also outgoing and friendly at your new job with the State Taxation Department.

____

____

____

____

____

____

____

____

You left home after high school and now when you go back home you want your parents to see you as different from the rebellious high school student you were. You want them to see you as a serious college student.

____

____

____

____

____

____

____

____

PART 2: DEFINING THE RELATIONSHIP

a. You want to indicate to co-workers that you are warm and friendly, but not available to date (you are married), flirt, or party.

b. You want to indicate to a sister or brother that the days of high school competitive sibling rivalry are over and that now (age 23) you want a close, respectful relationship in which you see each other as individuals.

c. You are extremely busy with school this semester but want your significant other/spouse to know how much you care about him/her even though you have little time this semester.

MMARY:

ıat types of nonverbal behaviors to you tend to rely on the most to manage impressions?

____

____

____

ggest ways that channels you don't frequently use could assist you in impression management.

____

____

____

NOTES ON NONVERBAL COMMUNICATION

NAME ______________________________

(CH)APTER 5. ACTIVITY 3: FUNCTIONS OF NONVERBAL COMMUNICATION

RPOSE:

. To identify the functions of nonverbal communication in context.

STRUCTIONS:

r each scenario below, tell which function of communication is being illustrated: repeating, ostituting, complementing, accenting, regulating, contradicting.

______________ **1.** The teacher pointed to the letter "s" on the board each time she pronounced it for the first-graders.

______________ **2.** The umpire shouted "safe" but made the sign for "out."

______________ **3.** The parent looked at the child with a look that clearly told her the topic of "chicken guts" was off limits at the table.

______________ **4.** Each time the politician said the word "taxes" he pounded on the table.

______________ **5.** Without saying a word, he just slipped his arm around her shoulders as if to tell the others they were together.

______________ **6.** First the instructor explained the karate form, then she demonstrated it.

. Are there some behaviors that you thought might fulfill more than one function? Which ones?

____

____

. Do you think the different functions are always distinctly different or are there ways in which they seem to overlap? Explain your answer.

____

____

____

ART 2

r each function, think of two examples (from your life, from films or stories) that illustrate that nction:

peating ______________________________

____

ibstituting ______________________________

____

mplementing ______________________________

____

accenting ____

____

regulating ____

____

contradicting ____

____

Many cartoons are based on contradicting nonverbal behaviors. Draw or tape such a cartoon here:

NAME ____________________

HAPTER 5. ACTIVITY 4: PRACTICING NONVERBAL SKILLS

JRPOSE:

1. To illustrate the richness of nonverbal communication.

ISTRUCTIONS:

1. Choose a partner.
2. Take turns saying the following sentences in each of the ways described.

1. Target person: your friend
   Verbal message: I'd like to go with you this weekend.
   Context: You frequently go away with each other, this is just routine, another weekend.
   What nonverbal channels are used most distinctly to convey the message this way?

   ____

   Context: You're hesitant. You've never gone with this friend on the weekend and you're suggesting it for the first time.
   What nonverbal channels are used most distinctly to convey the message this way?

   ____

   Context: Your friend is taking someone else with him/her, but you'd like to go. You wish you were the one invited to go with him/her.
   What nonverbal channels are used most distinctly to convey the message this way?

   ____

2. Target person: your spouse or significant other
   Verbal message: Do you want to go to the office party with me?
   Context: I don't really want to go; I'm too tired, and I sure hope you don't want to.
   What nonverbal channels are used most distinctly to convey the message this way?

   ____

   Context: I really want you to come with me because I'm excited about going.
   What nonverbal channels are used most distinctly to convey the message this way?

   ____

   Context: I have to go so I will, but I'm not excited about it. I'd like you to go with me so at least it isn't so miserable.
   What nonverbal channels are used most distinctly to convey the message this way?

   ____

3. Target person: your boss
   Verbal message: Do you think I'll get a promotion this year?
   Context: sincere, honest request for information
   What nonverbal channels are used most distinctly to convey the message this way?

   ____

Context: as if you're already convinced you won't, you're sad, disillusioned
What nonverbal channels are used most distinctly to convey the message this way?

____

Context: as if it's a big joke because you know for sure you won't (because you just did)
What nonverbal channels are used most distinctly to convey the message this way?

____

4. Target: your child
Verbal message: Well, you're free to choose the college and the course you want.
Context: Parents clearly want to convey the message that if the child doesn't do as they suggest, there will be consequences for him/her.
What nonverbal channels are used most distinctly to convey the message this way?

____

Context: Parents sincerely believe he/she will make the best choices for him/herself and they want child to make his/her own choices and they will respect their child and support whatever choices are made.
What nonverbal channels are used most distinctly to convey the message this way?

____

Context: Parents really don't care. They've been through this with two older children and just reall don't care what decision the child makes. They're just resigned to having no input.
What nonverbal channels are used most distinctly to convey the message this way?

____

DEBRIEF:

1. Which situations were hardest for you to convey? Why? ______________________

____

2. Which were easiest? Why?______________________________

____

3. List three **attitudes and feelings** (besides those in the text) that are easy to express nonverbally.

____

____

4. List three **ideas** that are difficult to express. ______________________

____

5. Give an example of a situation in which you think the verbal communication may be more important than nonverbal and explain why.

____

____

NAME ______________________________

[CH]APTER 5. ACTIVITY 5: EXPLORING THE WEB

[VA]RIETY IN NONVERBAL COMMUNICATION

[1]. Survey the table of contents of the latest issue of the *Journal of Nonverbal Behavior* at *http://198.199.133.62/jnvb.html.* List at least four current topics in nonverbal research.

____

____

____

____

____

[2]. Go to *http://www.eff.org/papers/eegtti/eeg_286.html* for an introduction to the use of smileys. What six categories of smileys do you find?

____

____

Look at the section on "emotional smileys." What generalizations can you make about the parts of the face frequently used in the attempt to express emotions online?

____

____

Can you generalize about which kinds of emotions are and aren't commonly expressed in emoticons?

____

[3]. Deception is closely related to nonverbal communication. Look at the bibliography on deception found at *http://cotton.uamont.edu/~roiger/biblio/decept.htmlx.*

What is the year of the oldest piece of research you find? ______________________________

What was the specific topic?

____

List the titles of at least five different journals in which deception research is published.

____

____

____

____

____

What inferences can you draw with regard to who is interested in research on deception?

4. Choose a particular topic of nonverbal communication that you would like to know more about. Locate the research page at *http://198.199.133.62/nonverbal.html.* What kind of information can you find on your topic here?

What are the titles of articles and specific journals that might inform your search?

5. Although largely an attempt to present information about videos on nonverbal communication, there are exercises built in to this Web site. Scroll to and look at the pictures and answer the questions in the online exercises in nonverbal communication found throughout at *http://zzyx.ucsc.edu/~archer/.* State three things you learned from these onscreen examples.

NAME ______________________________

[CH]APTER 5 SELF TEST

[M]ATCHING (KEY TERMS)

[Ma]tch each term listed on the left with its correct definition from the column on the right.

_____ **1.** affect blend
_____ **2.** chronemics
_____ **3.** disfluency
_____ **4.** emblems
_____ **5.** illustrators
_____ **6.** intimate distance
_____ **7.** kinesics
_____ **8.** manipulators
_____ **9.** mixed messages
_____ **10.** nonverbal communication
_____ **11.** paralanguage
_____ **12.** personal distance
_____ **13.** proxemics
_____ **14.** public distance
_____ **15.** social distance
_____ **16.** territory

a. messages expressed by other than linguistic means
b. nonlinguistic means of oral expression: rate, pitch, tone
c. nonverbal behaviors that accompany and support verbal messages
d. deliberate nonverbal behaviors with precise meanings, known to members of a cultural group
e. a nonlinguistic verbalization, such as um, er, ah
f. the combination of two or more expressions, each showing a different emotion
g. one of Hall's four distance zones, extending outward from 12 feet
h. study of body movement, gesture, and posture
i. one of Hall's four distance zones, ranging from skin contact to 18 inches
j. contradiction between a verbal message and one or more nonverbal cues
k. one of Hall's distance zones, ranging from 4 to 12 feet
l. fixed space that an individual assumes some right to occupy
m. the study of how people and animals use space
n. the study of how humans use and structure time
o. one of Hall's distance zones, ranging from 18 inches to 4 feet
p. movements in which one part of the body fidgets with another part

[M]ULTIPLE CHOICE

[C]hoose the BEST response from those listed.

1. Paralanguage refers to

a. the words spoken.
b. the various meanings in different languages.
c. the vocal messages of pitch, rate, and loudness.
d. languages passed on from parent to child.
e. none of the above

2. With regard to touch, which is true?

   a. Babies have never actually died from lack of touch.
   b. Touch is related to physical, but not mental, functioning.
   c. Touch seems to turn people off and decrease their compliance with requests.
   d. In mainstream U.S. culture, men touch men more than men touch women.
   e. Touch can communicate various messages ranging from aggression to affection.

3. According to research cited in the text,

   a. physical attractiveness has social and economic advantages.
   b. preschoolers didn't seem to like attractive children more than unattractive ones.
   c. teachers rated unattractive students as more intelligent and friendly than attractive ones.
   d. persons in uniforms seem less likely to influence or persuade people to act in certain ways.
   e. the longer we know someone, the more important that person's clothing is to our impressions of him/her.

4. The main point of the diversity reading in this chapter is that

   a. women have an advantage in having more styles available to them than men.
   b. men don't like women who dress like men.
   c. a woman is "marked" by the clothes she wears because she doesn't have the freedom of an "unmarked" style—it doesn't exist.
   d. men have a more difficult time blending in with their clothing—their type of suit always seems to draw attention.
   e. none of the above

5. According to Edward T. Hall, the distance at which most mainstream North American business is conducted is called ________.

   a. intimate
   b. personal
   c. social
   d. public
   e. none of the above

6. Which of these is a chronemic message which indicates status?

   a. Bosses dress more formally than employees.
   b. A person conducting an interview is usually conveying a less rigid posture than the person being interviewed.
   c. Students sit far apart at library tables to indicate their wish to study, not converse.
   d. Employees are rarely late for appointments with their supervisors, although supervisors may be late without penalties.
   e. Taller job candidates are more often chosen for jobs.

7. Which is true?

   a. Environments influence the kind of communication that takes place there.
   b. A particular environment can communicate the type of relationship desired.
   c. Environments can be designed to increase or decrease interaction.
   d. all of the above
   e. none of the above

8. Which is **not** a principle of nonverbal communication?

a. Communication occurs even when language is not used.
b. It is possible not to communicate nonverbally.
c. Nonverbal communication is ambiguous.
d. Nonverbal communication is culture-bound.
e. Nonverbal communication can serve various functions.

9. Which function of communication is illustrated by a person rolling his/her eyes while making a negative comment about another?

a. substituting
b. accenting
c. regulating
d. contradicting
e. repeating

0. Which of these factors should be considered when trying to make sense out of ambiguous nonverbal behavior?

a. context
b. history of the relationship
c. the other's mood
d. your feelings
e. all of the above

1. Marking your spot at a library or restaurant table by leaving a sweater and backpack illustrates a type of _________.

a. territory
b. chronemic
c. paralanguage
d. emblem
e. all of the above

2. In contrasting nonverbal and verbal messages, all of the following points were made **except** which one?

a. Nonverbal communication always involves multiple channels.
b. Nonverbal communication is continuous.
c. Much nonverbal communication is unconscious.
d. Nonverbal communication is much more consciously chosen than verbal communication.
e. All of the above points were made in the text.

3. Smiling a lot to convince people you are friendly, nodding to appear interested, and dressing to look professional are all types of nonverbal behavior that could be used for

a. identity management.
b. defining the relationship.
c. expressing attitudes and feelings.
d. all of the above
e. none of the above

14. Which of these statements almost requires verbal communication and would be difficult to expres nonverbally?

a. I'm tired and bored.
b. The party is exciting to me and I'm enjoying it.
c. The recent budget fiasco could have been prevented by better statistical analysis.
d. I'm confident about this opportunity to publicly address this group.
e. I'm in love with you and want to be near you.

15. Silence

a. has only one commonly accepted cultural meaning.
b. can be used to convey very different meanings, depending on the context.
c. rarely holds communication value or is given meaning by anyone.
d. all of the above
e. none of the above

TRUE/FALSE

Circle the T or F to indicate whether you believe the statement is true or false. If it is **true**, give a **reaso** or an **example**. If it is **false**, **explain** what would make it true.

T F **1.** Some nonverbal messages are vocal.

____

____

T F **2.** In trying to make sense out of nonverbal behavior, it is best to think of nonverbal behavio as clues to check out rather than absolute facts.

____

____

T F **3.** Most nonverbal messages are deliberate and intentional.

____

____

T F **4.** Unlike verbal messages which use many words at once, nonverbal communication utilizes only one channel at a time.

____

____

T F **5.** Research indicates that when people perceive inconsistencies between verbal and nonverbal messages, they usually believe the nonverbal one.

____

____

MPLETION

l in each of the blanks with a word from the list provided. Choose the BEST word for each sentence. ere are more words than you will use, but each word will be used only once.

ralanguage	chronemic	emblem	proxemic
nesic	disfluency		

1. "It is not sufficient to know what one ought to say, but one must also know **how to say it**." —Aristotle. Those words could be referring to the category of nonverbal communication called ____________________.

2. When a speaker says, "I **uh**, I'm glad to **uh** be here," this is an example of a __________________.

3. **Walking back and forth** in front of a group you are speaking to would be a ____________________ message.

4. Showing up **three hours late** for work is a type of ______________________ message.

5. Purposefully **standing closer** to the person you love to let others know you are at this party together is an example of a ______________________ message.

CHAPTER 5 ANSWERS TO SELF TEST

MATCHING (KEY TERMS)

1. f	**2.** n	**3.** e	**4.** d	**5.** c
6. i	**7.** h	**8.** p	**9.** j	**10.** a
11. b	**12.** o	**13.** m	**14.** g	**15.** k
16. l				

MULTIPLE CHOICE

1. c	**2.** e	**3.** a	**4.** c	**5.** c
6. d	**7.** d	**8.** b	**9.** b	**10.** e
11. a	**12.** d	**13.** d	**14.** c	**15.** b

TRUE/FALSE

1. T	**2.** T	**3.** F	**4.** F	**5.** T

COMPLETION

1. paralanguage	**2.** disfluency	**3.** kinesic	**4.** chronemic	**5.** proxemic

elated Reading

Vhat I Got When I Acted like a Guy," by Sheila Anne Feeney, *Redbook,* April 1995.

REVIEW:

'hat happens when a woman "acts like a guy"? The author of this reading spent three weeks finding ıt just how powerful our gender-bound expectations of nonverbal behavior are. Your text describes ıany culture-bound differences in nonverbal communication and here Sheila Feeney delineates some ell-documented nonverbal gender differences. She then proceeds to describe what happened when she roke many of the taboos regarding appropriate gender behavior. As you read, consider which types of onverbal communication taboos Ms. Feeney broke most often and what the functions of those types of ommunication were. Consider how, if the tables were turned and a guy acted like a gal, others would spond to him.

EVIEW:

1. What types of nonverbal communication did the author test out?
2. How does the author report feeling about her own experiment? Have you ever tried to act differently than you know you are expected to? With what results?
3. What kinds of feelings did the experiment generate in the author? In those she interacted with?
4. Speculate on reactions a male "acting like a gal" would get. In what ways do you think they'd be similar? Different?

NOTES ON NONVERBAL COMMUNICATION

Chapter 6
Understanding Human Relationships

ɪFTER STUDYING THIS CHAPTER, YOU WILL BETTER UNDERSTAND:

1. The characteristics that distinguish interpersonal relationships from impersonal ones.
2. The content and relational dimensions of every message.
3. The role of metacommunication in conveying relational messages.
4. Dimensions of and influences on intimacy in relationships.
5. Knapp's model of relational development and deterioration.
6. Dialectical perspectives in relational maintenance.
7. Reasons for self-disclosure and the Johari Window model of self-disclosure.
8. Characteristics of and guidelines for effective and appropriate self-disclosure.
9. The functions served by lies, equivocation, and hints.

FTER STUDYING THIS CHAPTER, YOU WILL BE BETTER ABLE TO:

1. Identify the extent to which relationships are interpersonal or impersonal, describe the level of satisfaction in a relationship, and suggest ways to increase satisfaction.
2. Identify the content and relational dimensions of a message.
3. Distinguish among types of intimacy and influences on intimacy.
4. Identify stages of relationships and the dialectical tensions present in relationships.
5. Identify the degree of self-disclosure in your relationships and the functions this disclosing communication serves.
6. Compose effective and appropriate disclosing messages.
7. Identify the types of nondisclosing communication you use, the functions these messages serve, and their ethical validity.

HAPTER 6 SKELETON OUTLINE

his outline can be a helpful study tool to assist you in seeing the order and sequence of the chapter and ıe relationship of ideas. Use it to take notes as you read and/or to add concepts presented in lecture.

I. CHARACTERISTICS OF INTERPERSONAL RELATIONSHIPS

- **A.** Definitions: Context vs. quality
  - **1.** Context, dyadic
  - **2.** Qualitative: impersonal vs. interpersonal
- **B.** Content and relational messages
  - **1.** Content messages
  - **2.** Relational messages
    - **a.** respect, inclusion, control, affection
    - **b.** expressed nonverbally
- **C.** Metacommunication
  - **1.** Benefits
    - **a.** resolving conflicts
    - **b.** reinforce positive
  - **2.** Risks of interpretation and analysis

II. INTIMACY AND DISTANCE

A. Dimensions of intimacy
  1. Physical
  2. Intellectual
  3. Emotional
  4. Shared activities

B. Male and female intimacy styles
  1. Emotional expression differences
  2. Activity: expressing or creating intimacy

C. Cultural influences
  1. Expectations and expression vary
  2. Collectivist cultures' variations

III. RELATIONAL DEVELOPMENT AND MAINTENANCE

A. Developmental models show stages of relationships.
  1. Initiating
  2. Experimenting
  3. Intensifying
  4. Integrating
  5. Bonding
  6. Differentiating
  7. Circumscribing
  8. Stagnating
  9. Avoiding
  10. Terminating

B. Dialectical perspectives
  1. Connection and autonomy (as in Desmond Morris's three stages)
    a.
    b.
    c.
  2. Openness and privacy
  3. Predictability and novelty
  4. Eight strategies for coping with dialectical tension
    a.
    b.
    c.
    d.
    e.
    f.
    g.
    h.

C. Characteristics of relational development and maintenance
  1. Change
  2. Movement

IV. SELF-DISCLOSURE IN INTERPERSONAL RELATIONSHIPS INVOLVES INFORMATION THAT IS DELIBERATE, SIGNIFICANT, UNKNOWN BY OTHERS. SOCIAL PENETRATION MODEL SHOWS BREADTH AND DEPTH.

A. Reasons for self-disclosure
  1. Catharsis
  2. Self-clarification
  3. Self-validation
  4. Reciprocity
  5. Impression management
  6. Relationship maintenance and enhancement
  7. Social control
  8. Manipulation

B. Johari Window model
   1. Open
   2. Blind
   3. Hidden
   4. Unknown

C. Characteristics of effective self-disclosure
   1. Influenced by culture
      a. appropriateness varies
      b. definition varies
      c. norms vary
   2. Usually occurs in dyads
   3. Usually is symmetrical
   4. Usually occurs incrementally
   5. Few high levels of disclosure
   6. Relatively scarce
   7. Usually occurs in positive relationships

D. Guidelines for appropriate self-disclosure
   1. Is the other person important to you?
   2. Is the risk of disclosing reasonable?
   3. Are the amount and type of disclosure appropriate?
   4. Is the disclosure relevant?
   5. Is the disclosure reciprocated?
   6. Will the effect be constructive?
   7. Is the disclosure clear and understandable?

E. Alternatives to self-disclosure
   1. Lies
   2. Equivocation
   3. Hinting
   4. Alternatives and ethics

HAPTER 6 KEY TERMS

is list of key terms corresponds to those in boldface in your text. Use these lines to write the finition and/or an example of the word on the line next to it.

tent message ______________________________

textual interpersonal communication ______________________________

lectical tensions ______________________________

ivocation ______________________________

personal communication ______________________________

interpersonal communication ______________________________

____

Johari Window ______________________________

____

metacommunication ______________________________

____

qualitative interpersonal communication ______________________________

____

relational maintenance ______________________________

____

relational message ______________________________

____

self-disclosure ______________________________

____

social penetration ______________________________

____

NAME ______________________________

[CH]APTER 6. ACTIVITY 1: CONTENT AND RELATIONAL MESSAGES

[PU]RPOSE:

[1]. To examine relational messages.

[IN]STRUCTIONS:

[Fo]r each situation, describe the types of relational messages you think are conveyed: inclusion, respect, [co]ntrol, affection.

[Ex]ample:

[Yo]ur out-of-town friends call and say, "We'll be passing through your town the night of the 22nd. We'd [lik]e to see you. Would it be convenient for us to visit or stay or would it be better if we stopped another [tim]e?"
What relational messages do you perceive?
The message seems high in respect because they care enough to call ahead which shows respect for [yo]ur schedule and life. It seems low in control because they aren't insisting on staying, thereby [co]ntrolling your time. There is a moderate amount of inclusion because they acknowledge it might be [ok]ay to stay; it's not out of the question as it would be for a business associate or new acquaintance, but [the]y don't automatically assume it's okay, either. Assuming one could stay might be more controlling. I [thi]nk there is affection and caring for the other's schedule. Really close friends and family might have [un]spoken agreements and assumptions about always staying with each other that imply a higher level of [aff]ection and inclusion.

[1]. A couple is discussing where to take their children and friends for pizza. The setting is loud and noisy. One parent says, "Okay, listen up. We're going to Pizza Hut. Jump in the car."

What relational messages do you perceive?

____

____

____

____

____

[2]. A new employee is on the job for the first day. As the lunch hour approaches, she/he says to the other employees in her/his area, "Well, where do we go for lunch?"

What relational messages do you perceive?

____

____

____

____

____

3. Your sister calls and starts telling you about a family reunion she's planning for this next summer. Before you've indicated whether or not you'll be able to attend, she says, "Everyone will be so glad to see you. And we can do some humorous decorations and you're always good with games for the kids. This will be so much fun."

   What relational messages do you perceive?

   ____

   ____

   ____

   ____

   ____

4. A co-worker says she's noticed how well you relate to everyone at work and asks if you'd consider running for local union steward.

   What relational messages do you perceive?

   ____

   ____

   ____

   ____

   ____

5. Your roommate leaves you a note saying, "I was hoping you'd be home before I had to go to class. I borrowed your blue sweatshirt for the evening. All my clothes were still wet. I hope you don't mind."

   What relational messages do you perceive?

   ____

   ____

   ____

   ____

   ____

NAME ______________________________

HAPTER 6. ACTIVITY 2: SELF-DISCLOSURE

URPOSES:

1. To understand the reasons for self-disclosure.
2. To distinguish between various purposes of self-disclosure.
3. To understand the relationship between our perception and others' disclosure.

ART 1

NSTRUCTIONS:

1. For each scenario, think about the various purposes for which the party described would self-disclose. Given the situation, what do you consider to be the most likely purposes for self-disclosing?
2. Write down the reasons why you think a person in that situation is most likely to self-disclose. Put a * by the one which you consider to be **the single most likely** reason for self-disclosure on the part of the person.
3. Share and compare your answers with your classmates.

1. Think about recent incidents when an American political figure who is in or campaigning for public office self-discloses to the press. In what ways might the self-disclosure be related to these reasons:

   catharsis ______________________________

   self-clarification ______________________________

   self-validation ______________________________

   reciprocity ______________________________

   impression management ______________________________

   relationship maintenance and enhancement ______________________________

   social control ______________________________

   manipulation ______________________________

2. Travelling across country by train, you meet someone you will be with for 24 hours on the train, but will probably not ever see after that. In this case self-disclosure is likely for the following purposes for these reasons:

   catharsis ______________________________

   self-clarification ______________________________

   self-validation ______________________________

   reciprocity ______________________________

   impression management ______________________________

   relationship maintenance and enhancement ______________________________

   social control ______________________________

   manipulation ______________________________

3. A son reveals to his mother that two years ago he paid for his girlfriend to have an abortion. In this case self-disclosure is likely for the following purposes for these reasons:

catharsis ______

self-clarification ______

self-validation ______

reciprocity ______

impression management ______

relationship maintenance and enhancement ______

social control ______

manipulation ______

4. A person is troubled by the fact that his father spent time in a mental institution. When getting involved in a relationship he doesn't want to share this information immediately [Hi! I'm John but before you get to know me you should know that . . .], but feels he is withholding something significant if he goes with someone very long without sharing this information. In this case self-disclosure is likely for these reasons:

catharsis ______

self-clarification ______

self-validation ______

reciprocity ______

impression management ______

relationship maintenance and enhancement ______

social control ______

manipulation ______

PART 2

1. In using self-disclosure for various reasons, in what kind of situations are you really aware of your own reasons for disclosure?

______

______

______

2. In what kind of situations might you not really be aware of your reasons for disclosing?

______

______

______

3. What difference does it make in a relationship, if someone self-discloses and you attribute his/her disclosure to one reason over another?

____

____

____

4. Can you think of recent examples of disclosures from public figures? Do different people's perceptions of them depend on their belief about the reasons for the self-disclosure?

____

____

____

6. In personal relationships, how could you use a perception check (see Chapter Two: description, interpretation, request for feedback) to more accurately understand another's motives for disclosure?

____

____

____

Reflect on your own self-disclosure:

When do you disclose or have you disclosed largely for reasons of

catharsis ____

self-clarification ____

self-validation ____

reciprocity ____

impression management ____

relationship maintenance and enhancement ____

social control ____

manipulation ____

NOTES ON UNDERSTANDING HUMAN RELATIONSHIPS

NAME ______________________________

HAPTER 6. ACTIVITY 3: RISKS AND REWARDS OF SELF-DISCLOSURE

RPOSE:

explore the risks and rewards of self-disclosure and its impact on relationships.

STRUCTIONS:

ead the following quotations and respond to each with your own thoughts and reactions.

1. "I can know only so much of myself as I have had the courage to confide to you. To the extent that I have hidden myself from you the meaning of your love will be diminished. I will forever fear that you love only the part of me that I have let you know; and that if you knew the real me, all of me, you would not love me. Love follows upon knowledge, and so you can love me only to the extent that I let you know me."—John Powell, *The Secret of Staying in Love*

   My first response to this quotation: ______________________________

   In your own words, what is this quotation saying about the impact of self-disclosure on relationships? About the risks of self-disclosure? About the rewards of self-disclosure?

   Do you agree or disagree with what is expressed here? Why? ______________________________

What words in the text lead you to believe the authors would agree or disagree with this quotation

2. "Most of us feel that others will not tolerate such emotional honesty [as disclosing feelings] in communication. We would rather defend our dishonesty on the grounds that it might hurt others, and having rationalized our phoniness into nobility, we settle for superficial relationships." —John Powell, *The Secret of Staying in Love*

My first response to this quotation:

In your own words, what does Powell mean by "rationalized our phoniness into nobility"? If we choose not to self-disclose our feelings, are we being phony?

Do you agree or disagree with what is expressed here? Why?

3. "There is a strong human temptation to judge people only in terms of these acts or masks [that we wear rather than disclosing]. It is all too rare that we are able to see through the sham and pretense of masks the insecure or wounded heart that is being camouflaged and protected from further injury. . . . We fail to realize that masks are worn only as long as they are needed."—John Powell, *Why Am I Afraid to Love?*

My first response to this quotation: ____________________

____

____

____

____

____

In your own words, what is this quotation saying about the need not to self-disclose if one is not comfortable doing so?

____

____

What "masks" do you see being worn most often? ____________________

____

Do you think they are worn because they need to be? Do you agree or disagree with what is expressed here? Why?

____

____

____

____

____

4. Jourard wrote, " . . . when you permit yourself to be known, you expose yourself not only to a lover's balm, but also to a hater's bombs. When he knows you, he knows just where to plant them for maximum effect."

My first response to this quotation: ____________________

____

____

____

____

____

In your own words, what does Jourard mean by "lover's balm" and "hater's bombs"? ______________

Do you agree or disagree with what is expressed here? Why? ______________

5. Calvin Coolidge (Silent Cal) once said, "I have never been hurt by anything I didn't say."

My first response to this quotation: ______________

Paraphrase the statement. ______________

Do you agree or disagree with what is expressed here? Why? ______________

NAME ______________________________

ɪAPTER 6. ACTIVITY 4: STAGES OF RELATIONSHIPS

RPOSES:

- To understand the stages of relationships.
- To correlate specific behaviors and words to stages of relationships.

STRUCTIONS:

oose a relationship that has ended. Can you identify behaviors that fit the characteristics of each ge? For each stage, list some behaviors that "proved" you were in that stage.

tiating ______________________________

perimenting ______________________________

ensifying ______________________________

egrating ______________________________

nding ______________________________

ferentiating ______________________________

cumscribing ______________________________

gnating ______________________________

oiding ______________________________

rminating ______________________________

a relationship is in the stagnating stage and you don't want it to terminate, what would you commend so that it moves into a "coming together" stage rather than a "coming apart" stage?

ample:

ck a new activity that neither of you has tried (line dancing, cross-country skiing, bridge) and learn it gether and see how you like it.

____

____

____

you tried these suggestions, what stage would you be moving into? ______________________________

NGS REFLECT RELATIONAL STAGES

om "Some Enchanted Evening" (initiating) to "Fifty Ways to Leave Your Lover" (terminating), titles d lyrics describe and differentiate stages of relationships. Try to come up with titles or lyrics that describe each stage of relationship. Some titles are deceiving. For instance, "I Said I Loved You But I Lied" may sound like terminating, but the lyrics make clear that it is "more than love" that is felt, making it a better candidate as a description of bonding. You may find this easier to do as a small-grou brainstorming session, especially when it comes to recalling lyrics.

initiating ____________________

experimenting ____________________

intensifying ____________________

integrating ____________________

bonding ____________________

differentiating ____________________

circumscribing ____________________

stagnating ____________________

avoiding ____________________

terminating ____________________

Share answers with classmates. Do you think that any particular types of music (country, rap, rock, show tunes) tend to have greater numbers of songs that reflect particular stages of relationships? For instance, do rock songs tend to speak more of initiating or bonding? Do country songs tend to speak more of bonding or terminating? Do certain types of music tend to emphasize initiating? Experimenting? Speculate on these questions. (Scholarly journals have articles that look systematical at themes from music. You might enjoy reporting on this now, or as part of a speech later in the cours

NAME ______________________________

APTER 6. ACTIVITY 5: INTIMACY AND DISTANCE

RPOSE:

. To explore the relationship between intimacy and autonomy in relationships.

STRUCTIONS:

ad the following quotations and respond to each with your own thoughts and reactions.

. "Each of us needs to establish our autonomy, or independence, and at the same time each of us desires intimacy with other people. We wish to be self-governing and independent individuals, but we also have a need to be a part of a group, to belong, to be needed by others, and to need them. We desire relational development and increased intimacy, but we are sometimes afraid of relationships developing too quickly. These seemingly conflicting goals exist in each of us." —Pearson, *Communication in the Family*

My first response to this quotation: ______________________________

In your own words, what is this quotation saying about everyone's needs? About time and intimacy?

Do you agree or disagree with what is expressed here? Why? ______

What words in the text lead you to believe the authors would agree or disagree with this quotation

2. "For her, intimacy without words is small comfort most of the time. It's not that she needs always to talk, but it's important to her to know what's going on inside him if she's to feel close. And it's equally important for her to believe he cares about what's going on inside her." —Rubin, *Intimate Strangers*

My first response to this quotation: ______

NAME ___________________________

In your own words, what is this quotation saying about gender differences regarding verbal and nonverbal expression of intimacy?

Do you agree or disagree with what is expressed here? Why?

What words in the text lead you to believe the authors would agree or disagree with this quotation?

3. "Wife: I say that foreplay begins in the morning.
Husband: It seems to me being sexual would make us closer, but she says it works the other way—if she felt closer, there'd be more sex." —Rubin, *Intimate Strangers*

My first response to this quotation:

In your own words, what is this quotation saying about talking and/or doing as paths to intimacy?

Do you agree or disagree with what is expressed here? Why?

What words in the text lead you to believe the authors would agree or disagree with this quotation?

4. "Being vulnerable in the presence of others—which we call intimacy—is closely related to maintaining commitment among family members. Family members reveal their vulnerabilities to one another, often with a sense of trust and usually with the hope that their vulnerabilities will not be used against them. For a family to live in the presence of each other's vulnerabilities and to stay intact, all members make an agreement (implicit or explicit) to maintain the family unit, at least at some minimum level." —Yerby, *Understanding Family Communication*

My first response to this quotation:

In your own words, what is this quotation saying about intimacy in families?

Do you agree or disagree with what is expressed here? Why?

What words in the text lead you to believe the authors would agree or disagree with this quotation?

5. "Most mothers receive more self-disclosure than fathers (Waterman 1979). Parents perceived as nurturing and supportive elicit more disclosure from children who find those encounters rewarding. College students are more likely to disclose more information more honestly to same-sex best friends than to either parent (Tardy, Hosman, and Bradac 1981)." —Galvin and Brommel, *Family Communication,* 4th ed.

My first response to this quotation:

In your own words, what is this quotation saying about intimacy in families and changes over time

In what ways does this quotation reflect or not reflect your experiences?

APTER 6. ACTIVITY 6: EXPLORING THE WEB

LF-DISCLOSURE AND THE JOHARI WINDOW

e text discusses the Johari Window as a model of self-disclosure. Go to the following site: *p://cotton.uamont.edu/~roiger/write/self-dis.html.* Appendix J.1 at that site provides a self-essment and scoring procedure that you can use to learn more about yourself with regard to self-closure levels and comfort. Complete this assessment.

. What are the labels and definitions of each label given to the four quadrants of the chart?

____

____

____

____

____

. The two columns you tally are "disclosure" and "feedback." What would you predict are the personality traits and behaviors of someone who would score high in the feedback area. Why?

____

____

____

____

____

. What kinds of careers would you predict persons who score high in disclosure choose? Why?

____

____

____

____

____

4. What would be the characteristics that you would predict they would choose for mates? Why?

____

____

____

____

____

5. Answer the same questions (3 and 4) for low-disclosers.

6. You might want to use the Interpersonal Competency Scale that categorizes motivation, knowledg and skill in interpersonal communication with subscales in adaptability, involvement, conversatio management, and empathy. It is found at *http://cotton.uamont.edu/%7Eroiger/write/competen.ht*

Record your scores here:

NAME ___________________________

[CH]APTER 6 SELF TEST

[M]ATCHING (KEY TERMS)

[Ma]tch each term listed on the left with its correct definition from the column on the right.

_____ **1.** content message
_____ **2.** contextual interpersonal communication
_____ **3.** dialectical tensions
_____ **4.** equivocation
_____ **5.** impersonal communication
_____ **6.** interpersonal communication
_____ **7.** Johari Window
_____ **8.** metacommunication
_____ **9.** qualitative interpersonal communication
_____ **10.** relational maintenance
_____ **11.** relational message
_____ **12.** self-disclosure
_____ **13.** social penetration

a. messages (usually relational) that refer to other messages or communication about communication
b. a model by Altman and Taylor to describe two dimensions of self-disclosure
c. a vague statement that can be interpreted in more than one way
d. a message that communicates information about the subject being discussed
e. behavior that treats others as objects rather than as individuals
f. the process of deliberately revealing information about oneself that is significant and would not be known by others
g. a model that describes the relationship between self-disclosure and self-awareness (blind, hidden areas)
h. gauging communication by the fact that it occurs in dyads
i. the message that expresses the social relationship between two or more individuals
j. communication in which the parties consider one another as unique individuals rather than as objects
k. conflicting desires in a relationship
l. interpersonal communication measured by its uniqueness and personal nature
m. communication aimed at keeping relationships functioning well

[M]ULTIPLE CHOICE

[Ch]oose the BEST response from those listed.

1. Which of these is a **qualitative** definition of interpersonal communication?

a. It involves two persons.
b. It occurs in dyads.
c. It involves each considering the other unique.
d. It is characterized as group or mass communication.
e. All of these are qualitative definitions.

2. The existence of dialectical tensions in relationships tends to contribute toward

a. a tendency of absolute sequential movement through the stages of relationships.
b. a tendency for back and forth movement across stages.
c. a tendency to stagnate at one stage.
d. all of the above
e. none of the above

3. Which is NOT a characteristic of stages of relationships according to Knapp?

a. Relationships exist in only one stage at a time.
b. Movement is rarely sequential and orderly.
c. Even strong relationships are rarely stable for long.
d. Movement is always to a new place, thus exhibiting flux.
e. Most relationships do go through these stages.

4. Self-disclosure is often gauged by which two factors?

a. depth and breadth
b. high and low
c. caring and respect
d. significance and privacy
e. stages and movement

5. You disclose to your parent the way you dumped your girl/boy friend in the hope that your parent will agree that you handled the situation well. This illustrates disclosure for which reason?

a. catharsis
b. self-clarification
c. self-validation
d. reciprocity
e. none of the above

6. In the film *Breakfast Club,* a group of teens are together for detention. One girl, Allison, seemingly self-discloses her bizarre sexual activity in an effort to get another teen, Claire, to disclose her sexual activity. Self-disclosing about oneself in an effort to get information from someone else may work because of which characteristic of self-disclosure?

a. Self-disclosure usually occurs in increments.
b. Self-disclosure usually is reciprocal.
c. Self-disclosure usually occurs in dyads.
d. all of the above
e. none of the above

7. In the Sydney Harris reading, "Polishing and Peeling," polishing is equated to ________.

a. authentic disclosure
b. reciprocity
c. impression management
d. self-clarification
e. relationship maintenance

8. Which is true of self-disclosure?

a. It is viewed essentially the same way around the world.
b. It rarely occurs incrementally.
c. It is strongly influenced by culture.
d. It usually occurs in large groups rather than dyads.
e. none of the above

9. Which of these represents a type of dialectical tension in relationships?

a. connection and autonomy
b. openness and privacy
c. predictability and novelty
d. all of these
e. none of these

F **4.** Hinting is a type of indirect behavior which can seek to get a desired response from the other and/or save the other from embarrassment.

____

____

F **5.** Men are more likely to see talk as a way to build intimacy; women are more likely to want to use shared activity to create intimacy.

____

____

MPLETION

in each of the blanks with a word from the list provided. Choose the BEST word for each sentence. ere are more words than you will use, but each word will be used only once.

ss	**metacommunication**	**impersonal**	**content**
uivocal	**intimate**	**relational**	

. Messages which tell us whether we are included, respected, or controlled are called ____________ messages.

. When considering the quality of communication, the opposite of interpersonal communication would be __________________ communication.

. __________________ communication may arise from intellectual or emotional closeness.

. Communication that has two equally plausible meanings is termed __________________ communication.

. Communication about communication is called __________________.

CHAPTER 6 ANSWERS TO SELF TEST

MATCHING I (KEY TERMS)

1. d	**2.** h	**3.** k	**4.** c	**5.** e
6. j	**7.** g	**8.** a	**9.** l	**10.** m
11. i	**12.** f	**13.** b		

MULTIPLE CHOICE

1. c	**2.** b	**3.** c	**4.** a	**5.** c
6. b	**7.** c	**8.** c	**9.** d	**10.** a
11. a	**12.** e	**13.** a	**14.** b	**15.** b
16. d				

MATCHING II (RELATIONAL STAGES)

1. c	**2.** a	**3.** e	**4.** d	**5.** b

TRUE/FALSE

1. F	**2.** F	**3.** T	**4.** T	**5.** F

COMPLETION

1. relational **2.** impersonal **3.** intimate **4.** equivocal
5. metacommunication

ELATED READING

Can Women and Men Be Friends?" Chapter 15 from *Among Friends: Who We Like, Why We Like Them, nd What We Do with Them,* by Letty Cottin Pogrebin (McGraw-Hill).

REVIEW:

ong before and certainly ever since the film *When Harry Met Sally,* one of the hottest topics of onversation has been "Can Women and Men Be Friends?" This chapter by Letty Cottin Pogrebin ddresses this question in the context of her larger subject, friends. The whole book is about friends: ow we make them, why we keep them, and how friendships develop. This chapter parallels many iemes from Chapter Six, including the importance of intimacy and distance, gender differences in itimacy, and stages of and self-disclosure in relationships. Whether or not you agree with her, her nalysis and summary of male/female friendships is fascinating and thought provoking.

EVIEW:

1. Can you think of any famous nonsexual friendships between men and women? Can you think of any (not so famous) from among your peers, family members, or acquaintances?
2. What did you find when you answered the questions at the beginning of the article? Were more of your answers the same sex as you or the opposite?
3. Do you agree that "male–female friendship is still the **exception** because equality—social equality—is still the exception"? (my boldface) Why or why not?
4. What is the author's "sociopolitical motive for wanting sex and friendship to remain distinct"? Do you agree that love and friendship can never be the same?
5. Paraphrase and respond to the summary or conclusion that Ms. Pogrebin presents.

NOTES ON UNDERSTANDING HUMAN RELATIONSHIPS

Chapter 7
Improving Interpersonal Relationships

FTER STUDYING THIS CHAPTER, YOU WILL BETTER UNDERSTAND:

1. The role of communication climate in interpersonal relationships.
2. Types of messages that contribute to confirming or disconfirming climates.
3. That conflict is unavoidable in interpersonal relationships.
4. Characteristics of nonassertive, directly aggressive, passive-aggressive, indirect, and assertive communication.
5. The influence of culture and gender on conflict styles.
6. The differences between win–lose, lose–lose, compromising, and win–win approaches to conflict resolution.

FTER STUDYING THIS CHAPTER, YOU WILL BE BETTER ABLE TO:

1. Identify disconfirming messages and replace them with confirming ones, using the Gibb categories of supportive communication.
2. Describe the degree to which you use nonassertive, directly aggressive, passive-aggressive, indirect, and assertive messages, and choose more satisfying responses as necessary.
3. Compose and deliver an assertive message, using the behavior-interpretation-feeling-consequence-intention format.
4. Apply the win–win approach to an interpersonal conflict.

HAPTER 7 SKELETON OUTLINE

his outline can be a helpful study tool to assist you in seeing the order and sequence of the chapter and e relationship of ideas. Use it to take notes as you read and/or to add concepts presented in lecture.

I. COMMUNICATION CLIMATES

- A. Confirming and disconfirming messages
  - 1. Confirming messages
    - a. recognition
    - b. acknowledgement
    - c. endorsement
  - 2. Disconfirming messages
    - a. disagreeing
    - b. ignoring
    - c. a matter of perception
- B. Development of communication climates
  - 1. Relational climates are formed verbally and nonverbally.
  - 2. Spirals reinforce climates.
    - a. escalatory conflict spirals
    - b. de-escalatory conflict spirals
- C. Creating positive communication climates (Gibb categories)
  - 1. Evaluation vs. description
    - a. "you" language
    - b. "I" language

2. Control vs. problem orientation
3. Strategy vs. spontaneity
4. Neutrality vs. empathy
5. Superiority vs. equality
6. Certainty vs. provisionalism

II. MANAGING INTERPERSONAL CONFLICT

A. The nature of conflict
  1. Expressed struggle
  2. Perceived incompatible goals
  3. Perceived scarce rewards
  4. Interdependence

B. Styles of expressing conflict
  1. Nonassertion
    a. avoidance
      (1) what is it?
      (2) when to use it?
    b. accommodation
      (1) what is it?
      (2) when to use it?
  2. Direct aggression
  3. Passive-aggression, "crazymaking"
    a. pseudo-accommodators
    b. guiltmakers
    c. jokers
    d. trivial tyrannizers
    e. withholders
  4. Indirect communication
    a. advantages
    b. disadvantages
  5. Assertion

C. Characteristics of an assertive message
  1. Behavioral description
  2. Interpretation of behavior
  3. Description of feelings
  4. Description of consequences
    a. what happens to you
    b. what happens to person spoken to
    c. what happens to others
  5. Statement of your intentions
    a. where you stand
    b. requests of others
    c. description of future action plan

D. Gender and conflict style
  1. Differences begin in childhood
    a. boys
    b. girls
  2. Differences continue as adults
    a. men
    b. women

E. Cultural influences on conflict
  1. Individualistic or collectivist
  2. High- or low-context
  3. Ethnicity

F. Methods of conflict resolution
  1. Win–lose
    a. power
    b. situations for use

2. Lose–lose
3. Compromise
4. Win–win
   a. goal
   b. situations for use

G. Steps in Win–win problem solving
   1. Identify problem and needs
   2. Make a date
   3. Describe problem and needs
   4. Partner checks back
   5. Solicit partner's needs
   6. Check your understanding of partner's needs
   7. Negotiate a solution
      a. identify and define the conflict
      b. generate a quantity of solutions
      c. evaluate solutions
      d. decide on best solution
   8. Follow up the solution

H. Letting go
   1. having a "Vesuvius"
   2. qualifications

IAPTER 7 KEY TERMS

is list of key terms corresponds to those in boldface in your text. Use these lines to write the finition and/or an example of the word on the line next to it.

ertion ______________________________

____

tainty ______________________________

____

mmunication climate ______________________________

____

npromise ______________________________

____

flict ______________________________

____

trolling message ______________________________

____

zymaking ______________________________

____

de-escalatory conflict spiral ____________________

____

descriptive communication ____________________

____

direct aggression ____________________

____

disconfirming response ____________________

____

empathy ____________________

____

equality ____________________

____

escalatory conflict spiral ____________________

____

evaluative communication ____________________

____

Gibb categories ____________________

____

"I" language ____________________

____

indirect communication ____________________

____

irrelevant response ____________________

____

lose–lose problem solving ____________________

____

neutrality ____________________

____

assertion ______________________________

____

blem orientation ______________________________

____

visionalism ______________________________

____

ral ______________________________

____

ntaneity ______________________________

____

ategy ______________________________

____

eriority ______________________________

____

–lose problem solving ______________________________

____

–win problem-solving ______________________________

____

u" language ______________________________

____

NOTES ON IMPROVING INTERPERSONAL RELATIONSHIPS

NAME ______________________________

HAPTER 7. ACTIVITY 1: RELATIONAL CLIMATES

URPOSE:

1. To investigate communication behaviors that can help create supportive climates.

NSTRUCTIONS:

1. For each situation, write down specific ways (verbal and nonverbal) that the person could behave to establish a confirming climate.
2. For each, tell why that would create a positive climate for you.

Situation	Describe several behaviors that, if engaged in by the **person in boldface,** would create a confirming climate for you.	Explain **why** you think these behaviors would create a supportive climate for you.
You have done poorly on a test and wish to talk to the **instructor** about it after class.	The instructor could make eye contact with me and listen to my concerns. He/she could refrain from looking at the clock and appearing hurried. Praise my effort and my taking time to come to the office.	By looking at and acknowledging me I'd feel valued. By being praised for taking time to come to the office, rather than hurried away, I'd feel appreciated.
You have just walked into a large room for a wedding reception. You know very few **people.**		
A new **supervisor** is taking over your work group and will meet employees for the first time.		
You are a patient at a new dental office and have arrived for your first visit. **(staff, hygienist, dentist)**		
You stop by to pick up a new classmate who isn't ready. The **parents** answer the door and ask you to sit in the living room to wait.		
You have volunteered in a group home for at-risk teens and have arrived to meet the **director,** tour the home, and have an orientation.		

NOTES ON IMPROVING INTERPERSONAL RELATIONSHIPS

NAME ______________________________

HAPTER 7. ACTIVITY 2: DEFENSIVE/SUPPORTIVE CLIMATES (GIBB)

IRPOSE:

1. To apply Gibb's categories to situations to analyze and improve communication.

ISTRUCTIONS:

r each item listed below, complete the forms as if you are the person speaking. Refer to the section in ur text on **Creating Positive Communication Climates**.

1. You and your brother both have 2-year-old children. You were at the park watching them play (your child was barefoot) and your brother said to you, "I never let Grigori (his child) go barefoot. It's really a health hazard for children and there are so many risks. I always take time to put shoes on him before we play outside."

   I would become defensive because I would perceive ____________________ (choose one or more Gibb category) on the part of my brother. Explain. ______________________________

   ____

   ____

   Alternative behavior based on Gibb categories: What could your brother have said or done differently?

   ____

   ____

   ____

   ____

2. A classmate looks over at your desk and says, "You still using Trapper Keepers? I used those in high school."

   I would become defensive because I would perceive ____________________ (choose one or more Gibb category) on the part of the classmate. Explain. ______________________________

   ____

   ____

   Alternative behavior based on Gibb categories:

   ____

   ____

   ____

   ____

3. You've been invited to a party by a co-worker. You arrive and the co-worker looks at you and says, "Oh, hi. I didn't know if you'd come." He/she then goes over to other guests. You know no one there.

I would become defensive because I would perceive ______________________ (choose one or mor

Gibb category) on the part of the co-worker. Explain. ______________________________________

____

____

Alternative behavior based on Gibb categories:

____

____

____

____

4. You are at work and helping a client while two others wait for your help. Your supervisor comes ou and says, "I'll see you in my office right now. We need to discuss your problems working with clients."

I would become defensive because I would perceive ______________________ (choose one or mor

Gibb category) on the part of ______________________. Explain. ____________________________

____

____

Alternative behavior based on Gibb categories:

____

____

____

____

NAME ____________________

HAPTER 7. ACTIVITY 3: PROBLEM SOLVING

JRPOSE:

1. To apply win–win problem solving.

ISTRUCTIONS:

hoose a conflict that you are comfortable addressing with someone. As a first practice, it is not lvisable to take the biggest nor the most emotional conflict in your life. First try working out a more anageable conflict. Plan how you would accomplish each step, then think carefully about your goals ad the other person involved as you consider how to work through these steps.

ENTIFY YOUR PROBLEM AND UNMET NEEDS

his stage involves much intrapersonal communication. Thinking about your needs necessitates giving a t of thought to your underlying relational needs. Write out what you believe is the problem and what our unmet needs are.

____

____

____

____

AKE A DATE

onsider timing. Is this a morning or an evening person? Are you watching nonverbals carefully? Has e other had time to think about this as you have? Will you suggest a time and a place free of stractions? What is your plan for making a date?

____

____

ESCRIBE YOUR PROBLEM AND NEEDS

/rite out some ways you could verbally describe your problem and needs in a nondefensive-provoking ay.

____

____

____

____

ARTNER CHECKS BACK

Vhat could you say or do to encourage your partner's understanding of you?

____

____

SOLICIT PARTNER'S NEEDS

What could you say or do to encourage your partner to express his/her needs?

____

____

____

CHECK YOUR UNDERSTANDING

After your partner has spoken, how could you check if you've understood his/her needs correctly? [Although you can't write out exact words without hearing your partner, write out some guidelines for yourself.]

____

____

____

NEGOTIATE A SOLUTION

Again, without specifics, you cannot do this in advance. Describe some guidelines for negotiating that you need to keep in mind.

____

____

____

FOLLOW UP THE SOLUTION

Remember to build in a follow-up so that neither of you feels this is unchangeable or locked in. What could you say or do to encourage follow-up?

____

____

____

As you look over your plan, what strengths and weaknesses do you see?

____

____

____

Will you likely approach this person about this conflict? Why or why not?

____

____

____

NAME ______________________________

HAPTER 7. ACTIVITY 4: WIN–WIN PROBLEM SOLVING

RPOSE:

1. To apply win–win problem solving.

STRUCTIONS:

1. For each step of the win–win problem-solving method, some possible statements to achieve that step are given. Read each one.
2. Which ones are in keeping with the spirit of win–win? Which statements might sabotage the process? Which ones create defensiveness? A disconfirming climate? Which ones are better than others in the group? Why? Rate each statement and be prepared to tell why.
   1 = excellent communication to achieve that goal
   2 = not the best, but it could work
   3 = poor communication, likely to create defensiveness or disconfirming climate

ENTIFY YOUR PROBLEM AND UNMET NEEDS

parent wanting a teen home by curfew.

______ I need to have you home at midnight.

______ I need to know you respect my authority.

______ I need to know that I can control you.

______ I don't sleep until I know you are safe, and I need to get up early.

roommate who frequently ends up cleaning up after others.

______ I need to feel valued and appreciated when I do clean up after you.

______ I need a clean room to bring my guests into.

______ I need to be able to go to the refrigerator and know that the food I bought is there for me.

______ I don't want to be taken for granted.

AKE A DATE

couple planning when to discuss whether or not their relationship will be exclusive.

______ Let's talk it over on the way to the party.

______ How about talking about it Monday night?

______ Let's go for a walk on the beach.

______ Let's talk Sunday at my mom's party.

ESCRIBE YOUR PROBLEM AND NEEDS

______ You just make me so mad when you won't ask your friends to be quiet while I'm studying.

______ I'd like to have a time set each night that I know your friends will be gone by or at least be quiet. When I come home from the library to study and it's noisy here, I don't get anything done.

______ You're always leaving dishes around and you're always asking to borrow my car and my clothes. Just show some respect.

PARTNER CHECKS BACK

_______ I've told you how it is for me, now you have to do the same.

_______ You'll ruin our chances of solving this if you don't put as much time and effort into this as I d

_______ Can't you just quickly say what you need?

SOLICIT PARTNER'S NEEDS

_______ So what do you want, anyway?

_______ Do you have to have everything your way?

_______ I'd like to hear how you see the situation and what you need.

CHECK YOUR UNDERSTANDING

_______ I think you're telling me that . . . but I'm not sure.

_______ I don't see why you think like that. That's not the way it is.

_______ So you're saying that you'd rather . . . than . . .?

NEGOTIATE A SOLUTION

_______ Let's think of as many ways as we can to solve this to both of our satisfactions.

_______ We're going to have to come up with something fast 'cause this discussing is driving me nuts

_______ Let's just do SOMETHING. If it doesn't work, we can try again.

_______ I'm sick and tired of talking about it. Let's just agree to something and be out of here.

FOLLOW UP THE SOLUTION

_______ Okay, if this doesn't work, let me know.

_______ If you're unhappy with this after six weeks, say something.

_______ Let's set a date for two weeks from now to sit down and see how this is working for us.

_______ Would you like to save our list of ideas, so if this doesn't work, we can try another solution?

NAME ______________________________

[CH]APTER 7. ACTIVITY 5: CONFLICT STYLES

[PU]RPOSES:

[1]. To become aware of the choices of response styles in any conflict situation.
[2]. To consider the various consequences of different response styles.

[IN]STRUCTIONS:

[1]. Assume you are the person in the situations given. Look at the possible response styles and FIRST fill in the response style for the way you would be most likely to handle that conflict [or the way you actually did handle a similar one]. Put a * in front of that response style and write down the results or probable results, both for you and for the other(s) involved.
[2]. Then look at the list of other possible response styles. Think of an option you have for each style. Write down a response that is an example of that style and note the probable results for you and others. Do the same for each item.

[1]. You just bought a new backpack at a well-known sporting goods store. It was expensive and you anticipated it would last through your college years. The first day you used it the zipper broke.

Nonassertive response: ______________________________

____

Probable results for you: ______________________________

____

Probable results for other(s): ______________________________

____

Directly aggressive response: ______________________________

____

Probable results for you: ______________________________

____

Probable results for other(s): ______________________________

____

Passive-aggressive response: ______________________________

____

Probable results for you: ______________________________

____

Probable results for other(s): ______________________________

____

Indirect communication response: ______________________________

____

Probable results for you: ______________________________

____

Probable results for other(s): ______________________________

____

Assertive response: ______________________________

____

Probable results for you: ______________________________

____

Probable results for other(s): ______________________________

____

2. An instructor continually places his/her hand on the back of your shirt as you work at the comput in class. You are uncomfortable with this.

Nonassertive response: ______________________________

____

Probable results for you: ______________________________

____

Probable results for other(s): ______________________________

____

Directly aggressive response: ______________________________

____

Probable results for you: ______________________________

____

Probable results for other(s): ______________________________

____

Passive-aggressive response: ______________________________

____

Probable results for you: ______________________________

____

Probable results for other(s): ______________________________

____

Indirect communication response: ______________________________

____

Probable results for you: ______________________________

____

Probable results for other(s): ______________________________

____

Assertive response: ______________________________

____

Probable results for you: ______________________________

____

Probable results for other(s): ______________________________

____

A classmate doesn't have a working car. A few weeks ago you gave him/her a ride on your way home. You casually said, "If you need a ride sometime, call me." You were thinking of occasionally, maybe a few times in the semester. Now, the classmate has called three or four times a week to ask for rides to different places.

Nonassertive response: ______________________________

____

Probable results for you: ______________________________

____

Probable results for other(s): ______________________________

____

Directly aggressive response: ______________________________

____

Probable results for you: ______________________________

____

Probable results for other(s): ______________________________

____

Passive-aggressive response: ______________________________

____

Probable results for you: ______________________________

____

Probable results for other(s): ______________________________

____

Indirect communication response: ______________________________

____

Probable results for you: ______________________________

____

Probable results for other(s): ______________________________

____

Assertive response: ______________________________

____

Probable results for you: ______________________________

____

Probable results for other(s): ______________________________

____

4. Describe a conflict situation that you or others have encountered.

Nonassertive response: ______________________________

____

Probable results for you: ______________________________

____

Probable results for other(s): ______________________________

____

Directly aggressive response: ____

____

Probable results for you: ____

____

Probable results for other(s): ____

____

Passive-aggressive response: ____

____

Probable results for you: ____

____

Probable results for other(s): ____

____

Indirect communication response: ____

____

Probable results for you: ____

____

Probable results for other(s): ____

____

Assertive response: ____

____

Probable results for you: ____

____

Probable results for other(s): ____

____

NOTES ON IMPROVING INTERPERSONAL RELATIONSHIPS

NAME ______________________________

HAPTER 7. ACTIVITY 6: EXPLORING THE WEB

ESOURCES FOR IMPROVING INTERPERSONAL COMMUNICATION

1. At *http://cotton.uamont.edu/~roiger/write/conflict.html* you will find an activity that asks you to read 25 proverbs and score them with regard to their desirability as conflict strategies. Scoring gives you insight into your preferred conflict resolution style(s). Print out a copy of the activity. Complete the exercise and score yours according to the directions given. (Read carefully and be certain you do the math correctly.)
2. List the five conflict styles as shown in this assessment with your score for each:

CONFLICT STYLE FROM ASSESSMENT	SCORE	IDENTICAL CATEGORY IN TEXT	TEXT DOESN'T HAVE IDENTICAL CATEGORY, BUT THIS SIMILAR ONE

3. What is your predominant conflict style according to the assessment?

____

4. Evaluate this assessment. Do you think this instrument is a valid measure of your conflict style? Why or why not?

____

____

____

____

5. What is the impact of a self-assessment? Predict what would happen if people closest to you completed the inventory **about** you.

____

____

____

6. Using a search engine, find at least four places that offer training, education, or consulting for improving interpersonal communication or dealing with conflict. Try key words: interpersonal communication or interpersonal conflict. List the name of the organization offering the training, its URL, and a description of the type of training it offers.

NAME OF ORGANIZATION	WEB SITE	TYPE OF TRAINING OFFERED

7. What kinds of **skills** seem to be advanced by these organizations as skills for dealing with conflict?

____

____

____

With relational issues?

____

____

____

If you have difficulty finding sites, you might begin with one of these to complete questions 6 and 7.

http://www.escape.ca/~rbacal/prevent.htm

http://www.queendom.com/navigate.html

NAME ______________________________

[CH]APTER 7 SELF TEST

[MA]TCHING (KEY TERMS)

[Ma]tch each term listed on the left with its correct definition from the column on the right.

1

_____ **1.** assertion

_____ **2.** certainty

_____ **3.** communication climate

_____ **4.** compromise

_____ **5.** conflict

_____ **6.** controlling message

_____ **7.** crazymaking

_____ **8.** de-escalatory conflict spiral

_____ **9.** descriptive communication

_____ **10.** direct aggression

_____ **11.** disconfirming response

_____ **12.** empathy

_____ **13.** equality

_____ **14.** escalatory conflict spiral

_____ **15.** evaluative communication

a. messages in which the sender judges the receiver in some way

b. an expressed struggle between at least two interdependent parties who perceive incompatible goals, scarce rewards, and interference from the other party in reaching their goals

c. messages that give an account of speaker's position without evaluating others

d. a communication spiral in which the parties lessen their interdependence, withdraw, and become less invested in the relationship

e. communication behavior that attacks the position and dignity of another person

f. direct expression of one's needs, thoughts, or feelings expressed in a way that does not attack the other's dignity

g. an approach to conflict resolution in which both parties attain part of what they want and give up part of what they want

h. the ability to project oneself into another person's point of view, so as to experience his/her thoughts and feelings

i. supportive communication that suggests others are of equivalent worth as human beings

j. a communication spiral in which one attack leads to another

k. message in which sender tries to impose some sort of outcome on the receiver

l. passive-aggressive messages sent in indirect ways that frustrate and confuse the recipient

m. the emotional tone of a relationship

n. messages that dogmatically imply that one's own position is correct and that the other's ideas are not worth considering

o. a response that expresses a lack of caring or respect for another person

Set 2

_______ **16.** Gibb categories

_______ **17.** "I" language

_______ **18.** indirect communication

_______ **19.** irrelevant response

_______ **20.** lose–lose problem solving

_______ **21.** neutrality

_______ **22.** nonassertion

_______ **23.** problem orientation

_______ **24.** provisionalism

_______ **25.** spiral

_______ **26.** spontaneity

_______ **27.** strategy

_______ **28.** superiority

_______ **29.** win–lose problem solving

_______ **30.** win–win problem solving

_______ **31.** "you" language

a. supportive communication behavior in which the communicator expresses honest and makes no attempt to manipulate the receiver

b. a defense-arousing behavior in which the communicator expresses indifference towa the other

c. a supportive style of communication in which the communicator expresses a willingness to consider the other person's position

d. an approach to conflict in which one party reaches its goal at the expense of the other'

e. the inability or unwillingness to express on thoughts or feelings when needed

f. an approach to conflict in which parties wo together to satisfy all their goals

g. hinting at a message instead of expressing thoughts and feelings in a straightforward way

h. disconfirming response in which one communicator's comments bear no relationship to the previous speaker's ideas

i. a defense-arousing style of communication which a person states or implies that he/sh is better than the other

j. defense-arousing style of communication in which the communicator tries to manipulat or trick the receiver

k. a supportive style of communication in which communicators focus on working together to solve problems instead of imposing solutions on each other

l. language that describes the communicator's position without evaluating others

m. language that judges another person, increasing the chance of defensive reaction

n. six sets of contrasting styles of behavior—one set describes a communication style likely to arouse defensiveness, the other set style likely to reduce it

o. an approach to conflict resolution in which neither party achieves its goals

p. reciprocal communication pattern in which each person's message reinforces the other's

ATCHING: GIBB OPPOSITES

tch each defensive-provoking term listed on the left with the term that Gibb describes as being nearly opposite.

_____ **1.** superiority
_____ **2.** control
_____ **3.** certainty
_____ **4.** neutrality
_____ **5.** evaluation
_____ **6.** strategy

a. description
b. empathy
c. equality
d. provisionalism
e. spontaneity
f. problem orientation

ATCHING: CLEAR MESSAGES ELEMENTS

tch each item on the left with the part of a clear message that it represents. They can be used more n once. The boldfaced part of the item is the part to pay attention to; the other is there for ckground.

. behavioral description
. interpretation
. feelings
. consequences
. intentions

_______ **1.** When you came over without calling, . . .

_______ **2.** **I felt uncomfortable** because I don't have time for you.

_______ **3.** Tonight I came home and found the kitchen clean, . . .

_______ **4.** so I have time to cook you a great dinner.

_______ **5.** (When you say you love me), **I feel appreciated and loved.**

_______ **6.** (When you called me "sweetie" in the office), **I thought you were trying to show your power over me.**

_______ **7.** I think you're being rude.

_______ **8.** I don't want you to ignore my sister anymore.

_______ **9.** When my sister is here and you don't say hello, . . .

_______ **10.** I have to apologize to her for your behavior.

ULTIPLE CHOICE

oose the BEST response from those listed.

. Which of these is NOT a confirming response?

a. praise
b. compliment
c. pseudolistening
d. acknowledging
e. all of the above

2. A de-escalatory conflict spiral

a. refers to a positive, nondestructive climate.
b. involves intense fights.
c. refers to less involvement and greater withdrawal.
d. produces greater involvement in the relationship.
e. none of the above

3. Spontaneity, as used by Gibb, is closest to which of the following?

a. spur-of-the-moment
b. unplanned
c. honest
d. uncaring
e. fair

4. Practicing the communication behaviors Gibb labels supportive, rather than those labeled defensive,

a. increases the chance of a constructive relationship.
b. increases the chance of a more positive relationship if it is already positive, but decreases the chance of a positive relationship if it is already defensive.
c. increases the chances of you feeling better about yourself with regard to this relationship.
d. both b and c
e. both a and c

5. Neutrality, as used by Gibb, is closest to which of the following?

a. mean-spirited
b. unplanned
c. kind
d. indifferent
e. fair

6. Accommodation and avoidance are both forms of ________.

a. assertion
b. nonassertion
c. crazymaking
d. passive aggression
e. direct aggression

7. Crazymaking is synonymous with ________.

a. assertion
b. nonassertion
c. indirect communication
d. passive aggression
e. direct aggression

8. Guiltmakers, jokers, trivial tyrannizers, and withholders are all engaged in behaviors called ________.

a. assertion
b. nonassertion
c. crazymaking
d. indirect communication
e. direct aggression

Which is NOT true of assertive communication?

a. It expresses feelings clearly and directly.
b. It does not judge or dictate to others.
c. It treats others with respect and dignity.
d. It helps communicators maintain better feelings about themselves.
e. It ensures communicators can always get what they want.

When using an assertive message, the text stresses that you

a. put the message in the order given in the text.
b. put intentions first so you're not seen as manipulative.
c. choose the best order for your particular situation and goal.
d. keep each element in a separate sentence.
e. both c and d

Most theorists believe that gender differences in conflict style stem from ________.

a. biology/heredity
b. parental influence
c. school and society
d. socialization
e. all but a

The conflict resolution method and assertive message skills taught in this chapter would work well when communicating

a. in Asian cultures.
b. among Latin Americans.
c. in predominantly Euroamerican work environments.
d. all of the above
e. none of the above

Which of these is NOT typical of a win–lose style?

a. courts awarding sole custody to one parent, when both want custody of a child
b. the World Series or Super Bowl
c. political election campaigns
d. job sharing/flex time
e. all indicate a win–lose style

Susan needs to be in class from 6 to 9. Demetri needs to be at a meeting from 6:30 to 8:30. They have only one car. If Demetri drops Susan off at class and picks her up, so both get to be where they need to be, and it works better for Susan not to have to park in a student parking lot far from the class, this solution could be called ________.

a. win–win
b. win–lose
c. compromise
d. lose–lose
e. none of the above

A person from a low-context culture

a. will likely hint at a problem, rather than come right out and speak of it.
b. will usually speak directly and assertively.
c. will usually not say "no" right away to another person's request.
d. will not risk embarrassing the other person by direct talk.
e. None of the above reflects a low-context cultural stance.

TRUE/FALSE

Circle the T or F to indicate whether you believe the statement is true or false. If it is **true,** give a **reaso** or an **example.** If it is **false, explain** what would make it true.

T F **1.** In order for "expressed struggle" to exist, the struggle must be verbalized.

____

____

T F **2.** A communication climate is determined by the amount of talk that exists in a relationshi

____

____

T F **3.** Conflict exists when there is expressed struggle, interdependence, perceived incompatibl goals, scarce rewards, and interference with goals.

____

____

T F **4.** While culture and gender influence speech patterns, researchers have not found any genc or culture differences with regard to how persons view and handle conflict.

____

____

T F **5.** Win–win is the most widely used method of conflict resolution in our society.

____

____

COMPLETION

Fill in each of the blanks with a word from the list provided. Choose the BEST word for each sentence. There are more words than you will use, but each word will be used only once.

valued	**neutrality**	**power**	**superiority**
needs	**empathy**	**empowered**	

1. Communication climate is determined by the degree to which people feel they are

____________________.

2. ____________________ is the most distinguishing characteristic of win–lose problem solving.

3. In order to frame a conflict in such a way that a win–win solution is likely, it is necessary to think in terms of the ____________________ of each person.

4. This quotation by Shaw is closest to the Gibb category of ____________________: "The worst sin toward our fellow creatures is not to hate them, but to be indifferent to them; that's the essence of inhumanity."

5. "In the age of e-mail, supercomputer power on the desktop, the Internet, and the raucous global village, attentiveness—a token of human kindness—is the greatest gift we can give someone." —Tom Peters, *The Pursuit of WOW!* This quotation is closest to what Gibb describes as ____________________.

CHAPTER 7 ANSWERS TO SELF TEST

MATCHING (KEY TERMS)

Set 1

1. f **2.** n **3.** m **4.** g **5.** b
6. k **7.** l **8.** d **9.** c **10.** e
11. o **12.** h **13.** i **14.** j **15.** a

Set 2

16. n **17.** l **18.** g **19.** h **20.** o
21. b **22.** e **23.** k **24.** c **25.** p
26. a **27.** j **28.** i **29.** d **30.** f
31. m

MATCHING: GIBB OPPOSITES

1. c **2.** f **3.** d **4.** b **5.** a
6. e

MATCHING: CLEAR MESSAGES ELEMENTS

1. a **2.** c **3.** a **4.** d **5.** c
6. b **7.** b **8.** e **9.** a **10.** d

MULTIPLE CHOICE

1. c **2.** c **3.** c **4.** e **5.** d
6. b **7.** d **8.** c **9.** e **10.** c
11. d **12.** c **13.** d **14.** a **15.** b

TRUE/FALSE

1. F **2.** F **3.** T **4.** F **5.** F

COMPLETION

1. valued **2.** power **3.** needs **4.** neutrality **5.** empathy

.elated Reading

When Black Women Talk with White Women: Why Dialogues Are Difficult," by Marsha Houston, *Our ɔices: Essays in Culture, Ethnicity, and Communication: An Intercultural Anthology,* edited by lberto Gonzalez, Marsha Houston, and Victoria Chen (Roxbury Publishing Company, 1994).

REVIEW:

hapter 7 takes a broad view of avenues to improve interpersonal relationships of various sorts. This ꞓading focuses more narrowly on a particular relationship: friendships between black and white omen. Author Marsha Houston provides interesting correlations to previous chapters on the role of ꞓlf-concept, perception, and language in sustaining or undermining friendships. Her advice in this rticle can be seen as means of creating more confirming messages and more positive climates in black nd white women's friendships, thus perhaps avoiding at least one type of interpersonal conflict. As you ꞓad, consider how your experiences or perceptions of black and white women influence your view of is author's analysis of the difficulties of dialogue between black and white women.

EVIEW:

1. Imagine this article written by a Euroamerican woman. Would any of the three pieces of advice be appropriate for Euroamerican women (or men) for interracial friendships? Why or why not?
2. The author states that she does not intend to give a "definitive or an exhaustive analysis" of interracial women's talk. Would you add anything to her understanding of the two reasons why black women often find conversations with white women unsatisfying and/or the three statements she suggests avoiding?
3. How do you think an article on interracial men's talk would be similar to or different from this article?
4. Do your experiences validate or refute the author's conclusions?

NOTES ON IMPROVING INTERPERSONAL RELATIONSHIPS

Chapter 8
The Nature of Groups

FTER STUDYING THIS CHAPTER, YOU WILL BETTER UNDERSTAND:

1. The characteristics that distinguish groups from other collections of people.
2. The types of goals that operate in groups.
3. The various types of groups.
4. The characteristics of groups described in this chapter.
5. The advantages and disadvantages of the decision-making methods introduced in this chapter.
6. The cultural influences that shape communication in groups.

FTER STUDYING THIS CHAPTER, YOU WILL BE BETTER ABLE TO:

1. Identify the groups you presently belong to and those you are likely to join in the future.
2. List the personal and group goals in groups you observe or belong to.
3. Identify the norms, roles, and interaction patterns in groups you observe or belong to.
4. Choose the most effective decision-making methods for a group task.

IAPTER 8 SKELETON OUTLINE

iis outline can be a helpful study tool to assist you in seeing the order and sequence of the chapter and e relationship of ideas. Use it to take notes as you read and/or to add concepts presented in lecture.

I. WHAT IS A GROUP?

- **A.** Interaction
- **B.** Time
- **C.** Size
- **D.** Goals

I. GOALS OF GROUPS AND MEMBERS

- **A.** Individual goals
  1. Task orientation
  2. Social orientation
- **B.** Group goals
  1. Relationship between group/individual goals
  2. Hidden agenda

I. TYPES OF GROUPS

- **A.** Learning groups
- **B.** Growth groups
- **C.** Problem-solving groups
- **D.** Social groups

IV. CHARACTERISTICS OF GROUPS

- **A.** Rules and norms
  - **1.** Rules
  - **2.** Norms
    - **a.** social
    - **b.** procedural
    - **c.** task
    - **d.** identification of
      - **(1)** habitual behaviors
      - **(2)** punishment for violation
- **B.** Roles
  - **1.** Formal
  - **2.** Informal
  - **3.** Task
  - **4.** Social
  - **5.** Dysfunctional
  - **6.** Role emergence
  - **7.** Role problems and solutions
    - **a.** under filled
    - **b.** over filled
    - **c.** role fixation
- **C.** Patterns of interaction
  - **1.** Mathematical
  - **2.** Sociograms
  - **3.** Physical environment
  - **4.** Networks
    - **a.** all-channel
    - **b.** chain
    - **c.** wheel
    - **d.** gatekeeper
- **D.** Decision-making methods
  - **1.** Consensus
  - **2.** Majority
  - **3.** Expert
  - **4.** Minority
  - **5.** Authority

V. CULTURAL INFLUENCES ON GROUP COMMUNICATION

- **A.** Individualism vs. collectivism
  - **1.** Individualistic
  - **2.** Collectivistic
- **B.** Power distance
  - **1.** Low
  - **2.** High
- **C.** Uncertainty avoidance
  - **1.** Low
  - **2.** High
- **D.** Task vs. social orientation
  - **1.** High task
  - **2.** High social

HAPTER 8 KEY TERMS

his list of key terms corresponds to those in boldface in your text. Use these lines to write the efinition and/or an example of the word on the line next to it.

l-channel network ______________________________

____

ain network ______________________________

____

llectivistic orientation ______________________________

____

nsensus ______________________________

____

sfunctional role ______________________________

____

nctional role ______________________________

____

tekeeper ______________________________

____

oup ______________________________

____

oup goals ______________________________

____

owth group ______________________________

____

dden agenda ______________________________

____

dividual goals ______________________________

____

dividualistic orientation ______________________________

____

learning group ______________________________

____

norms ______________________________

____

power distance ______________________________

____

problem-solving group ______________________________

____

procedural norm ______________________________

____

role fixation ______________________________

____

roles ______________________________

____

rules ______________________________

____

social goals ______________________________

____

social group ______________________________

____

social norms ______________________________

____

social orientation ______________________________

____

social roles ______________________________

____

sociogram ______________________________

____

.sk norms ______________________________

____

.sk orientation ______________________________

____

.sk roles ______________________________

____

.sk-related goals ______________________________

____

ncertainty avoidance ______________________________

____

heel network ______________________________

____

NOTES ON THE NATURE OF GROUPS

NAME ______________________________

HAPTER 8. ACTIVITY 1: GROUP CHARACTERISTICS AND GOALS

URPOSES:

1. To identify characteristics of groups one belongs to.
2. To analyze goals for groups one has membership in.

NSTRUCTIONS:

1. Choose three groups that you are a part of. Try to choose groups that fit in different categories (problem-solving, learning, growth, social).
2. Analyze each by filling in the information below.

roup 1. Name of group ______________________________

escribe the group's interaction over time: Nature and amount of interaction? Over what period of time o/have they interact(ed)?

____

____

escribe the size of the group. ______________________________

____

escribe the goals of the group.

a. What are your individual task goals in the group? ______________________________

____

____

b. What are your individual social goals in the group? ______________________________

____

____

escribe the group goals and how you know these are the group goals.

____

____

o you or others have hidden agendas that you are aware of? If so, how do they affect the group?

____

____

o your individual goals and the group goals harmonize or is there conflict between the two sets of goals?

____

____

As what category (learning, growth, problem-solving, social) would you characterize this group? Explai why.

____

____

Group 2. Name of group ______________________________

Describe the group's interaction over time: Nature and amount of interaction? Over what period of tim do/have they interact(ed)?

____

____

Describe the size of the group. ______________________________

____

Describe the goals of the group.

a. What are your individual task goals in the group? ______________________________

____

____

b. What are your individual social goals in the group? ______________________________

____

____

Describe the group goals and how you know these are the group goals.

____

____

Do you or others have hidden agendas that you are aware of? If so, how do they affect the group?

____

____

Do your individual goals and the group goals harmonize or is there conflict between the two sets of goal

____

____

As what category (learning, growth, problem-solving, social) would you characterize this group? Explai why.

____

____

oup 3. Name of group ______________________

escribe the group's interaction over time: Nature and amount of interaction? Over what period of time
/have they interact(ed)?

____

____

escribe the size of the group. ______________________

____

escribe the goals of the group.

a. What are your individual task goals in the group? ______________________

____

____

b. What are your individual social goals in the group? ______________________

____

____

escribe the group goals and how you know these are the group goals.

____

____

o you or others have hidden agendas that you are aware of? If so, how do they affect the group?

____

____

o your individual goals and the group goals harmonize or is there conflict between the two sets of goals?

____

____

s what category (learning, growth, problem-solving, social) would you characterize this group? Explain
hy.

____

____

____

DISCUSSION/CONCLUSIONS

What do you think is a correlation between the type of group (learning, growth, problem-solving, socia and the presence or absence of hidden agendas? Do you think hidden agendas are more or less likely i certain groups?

Are your social goals different depending on the type of group you belong to?

Are there some groups you don't currently belong to but would like to? What groups would you join if you could?

Why?

Are there any groups that you belong to but would like to be out of? Why? Are those groups failing to meet needs of yours? Which ones?

What was the most productive group you were ever part of? What made it so? Try to identify the facto that contributed to its productivity. Was the group's productivity at all related to group and individual goals?

What was the most ineffective group you were ever part of? Why was it so bad? Can you identify facto that made it ineffective? Was the group's productivity related to group and individual goals?

NAME ______________________________

HAPTER 8. ACTIVITY 2: GROUP NORMS AND RULES

RPOSES:

.. To distinguish between rules and norms.
. To identify norms through observing behavior.

STRUCTIONS:

hoose two groups you belong to. For each, you will focus on the rules and norms of the group. Try to scribe behaviors.

Sample: work group at fast-food restaurant **List several explicit (written) rules of the group.**	**1.** Show up on time or be docked pay. **2.** Wear the uniform given to you. **3.** Don't leave until clean-up is done, even if shift is over.
Describe a social norm.	**1.** Everyone says "hi" to everyone when they come on to a shift. **2.** Another strong social norm is if a new female employee starts working, the guys see who she talks to the most. The others are not to try to date her or get close to her. They are not to flirt, etc., if she shows interest in someone else.
What behaviors in the group reinforce following the norm or punish violations of the norm?	**1.** If someone doesn't say "hi" to someone else, he/she usually shouts to him/her, "Hey, what's the matter? You gonna say 'hi' today or not?" **2.** Everyone will talk about you ("Hey, John's trying to take over") or tease you if you violate the norm.
Describe a procedural norm.	The procedural norm is pretty much by seniority. For jobs we're supposed to share, those who've been there longest say whether they'll do grill or window or drive-up; the rest take what's left by pecking order.
What behaviors reinforce following the norm or punish violations of the norm?	Everyone just follows this. If a new person says what he/she would like before a "senior" speaks, everyone pretty much ignores the person and listens to the next senior person.
Describe a task norm.	Problems among employees are handled one-to-one. Don't go to the manager for "minor" concerns.
What behaviors reinforce following the norm or punish violations of the norm?	If employees go to the manager with a "minor" problem (they don't like their hours, they want a different shift), the others ostracize them. It's understood that you take what you get.

GROUP 1:	
List several explicit (written) rules of the group.	1. 2. 3.
Describe a social norm.	
What behaviors in the group reinforce following the norm or punish violations of the norm?	
Describe a procedural norm.	
What behaviors in the group reinforce following the norm or punish violations of the norm?	
Describe a task norm.	
What behaviors in the group reinforce following the norm or punish violations of the norm?	

GROUP 2:	
List several explicit (written) rules of the group.	1. 2. 3.
Describe a social norm.	
What behaviors in the group reinforce following the norm or punish violations of the norm?	
Describe a procedural norm.	
What behaviors in the group reinforce following the norm or punish violations of the norm?	
Describe a task norm.	
What behaviors in the group reinforce following the norm or punish violations of the norm?	

NOTES ON THE NATURE OF GROUPS

NAME ______________________________

APTER 8. ACTIVITY 3: GROUP ROLES

RPOSES:

1. To identify roles in groups.
2. To be able to describe behaviors characteristic of various roles.

STRUCTIONS:

1. Form groups of eight to ten. Half of the members should designate themselves as A's and half as B's. For the first discussion, A's will be group participants; B's will be observers. One B should take on the additional role of timekeeper. For the second discussion, roles will be switched.
2. Sit in "fish bowl" style, with the A's seated in a small circle as close to each other as possible, while B's surround that group so they can observe.
3. A's should choose one of the "Group Exercises" below. After 10 minutes, one of the B's will inform them that their time is up.
4. During the discussion, B's should use the observation forms and watch for evidence of different roles being performed by various group members. Jot down behaviors that seem to characterize various roles. Your job is to report **observations, not evaluations** of group members and activities.
5. After the discussion, B's should report their observations to the whole group (A's and B's).
6. Discuss the questions at the bottom of this page as a whole group.

ROUP EXERCISES

1. Hypothetical situation: The instructor is willing to add between 1 and 50 points (out of 1,000) to students' grades for notable class participation this semester. Devise a plan to determine the number of participation points each student should receive. Your job is to come up with a plan to assign points, not to assign them. The plan should be a workable, fair plan that you can present to the instructor.
2. Money has been allocated for five new student support positions at your college. These are not instructor positions, but may be any type of support services. What student support services are most needed? Provide a plan for use of these funds.
3. Assume that this group is a student liaison committee to facilitate communication between students and administration. There is no additional money. Create a directive to the administration citing the three most significant things the administration could do that would benefit students at no additional cost.

OST-OBSERVATION DISCUSSION QUESTIONS FOR THE WHOLE GROUP

1. Which roles did each person fill?
2. Which roles were not filled?
3. Which roles were competed for?
4. Why might group members see their own behaviors differently from each other?
5. Why might observers and group members "see" behaviors differently?
6. Was there any role fixation?
7. For participants: Which roles were you comfortable in? Did you have to stretch yourself to fulfill any roles that aren't part of your usual repertoire? Which ones?
8. What decision-making method(s) was (were) used by the group?

Group Roles Observation

TASK ROLES IN GROUPS	DESCRIBE BEHAVIORS HERE (VERBAL/NONVERBAL)
1. **Initiator/contributor** (proposes ideas, solutions, suggestions)	
2. **Information seeker** (asks others for relevant information)	
3. **Information giver** (offers facts, relevant evidence)	
4. **Opinion giver** (states opinions and beliefs)	
5. **Opinion seeker** (asks others for opinions/beliefs)	
6. **Elaborator/clarifier** (expands ideas, shows how idea would work for group)	
7. **Coordinator** (clarifies relationships among contributions)	
8. **Diagnostician** (assesses group behavior: "We spend a lot of time . . .")	
9. **Orienter/summarizer** (reviews and identifies themes in what's been said)	
10. **Energizer** (invigorates, enthuses group for task)	
11. **Procedure developer** (attends to seating, equipment)	
12. **Secretary** (keeps notes)	
13. **Evaluator/critic** (constructive analysis of accomplishment)	
Other comments	

SOCIAL/MAINTENANCE ROLES IN GROUPS	DESCRIBE BEHAVIORS HERE (VERBAL/NONVERBAL) (INCLUDE NAMES OF PARTICIPANTS DISPLAYING BEHAVIORS)
1. **Supporter/encourager** (praises, accepts others, warmth and recognition freely given)	
2. **Harmonizer** (mediates interpersonal conflicts and reduces tensions among group members)	
3. **Tension reliever** (helps relieve anxiety and pressures in group)	
4. **Conciliator** (offers options if his/her ideas are creating conflict, maintains cohesion)	
5. **Gatekeeper** (keeps channels open; encourages interaction) speaks: "Bill hasn't had a turn. John, before you speak again could we hear from Mary?")	
6. **Feeling expresser** (makes feelings, moods of group and self explicit)	
7. **Follower** (passive acceptance of group movement)	

DYSFUNCTIONAL ROLES	
1. **Blocker** (prevents progress by raising objections constantly)	
2. **Aggressor** (aggressively questions others' motives or competence)	
3. **Deserter** (refuses to participate, take stand, or respond to others)	
4. **Dominator** (interrupts, monopolizes)	
5. **Recognition seeker** (boasts, brags, and calls attention to self and accomplishments inappropriately)	
6. **Joker** (shows lack of involvement by clowning or joking in excess)	
7. **Cynic** (shoots down ideas, discounts chances for success)	

Individual Summary:

Roles that I am most comfortable with in most groups:

Why are these roles comfortable for you?

Roles that I am least comfortable with:

Why?

What would it take to feel comfortable with some of these roles?

Roles I may compete for:

In what circumstances:

NAME ______________________

APTER 8. ACTIVITY 4: GROUP DECISION MAKING

RPOSE:

apply group decision-making skills.

STRUCTIONS:

rt 1

ad each scenario. For each, decide which decision-making method you would recommend and why.

cision-making methods: consensus, majority, expert, minority, authority

1. The budget for the (Speech) Communication Department has been increased. You are on a student committee to report to the department. Your task is to create and prioritize a list of items that, if funded, would best satisfy student needs.

   Decision-making method recommended: ______________________

   Reasons: ______________________

   ____

   ____

2. You are asked to serve on an ad hoc committee of the student government. Money has been allocated for grounds and physical plant improvements at your college. The committee is to decide what improvements in the physical environment would be most beneficial for students' academic, social, and safety needs. You are to prepare a concrete list of ideas and prioritize them for student government.

   Decision-making method recommended: ______________________

   Reasons: ______________________

   ____

   ____

3. You are part of a campus organization which is going to have a fund-raiser. The decision about what type of fund-raiser to hold needs to be made.

   Decision-making method recommended: ______________________

   Reasons: ______________________

   ____

   ____

4. Your family is trying to decide what kind of party to give for your grandparents' 50th wedding anniversary.

   Decision-making method recommended: ______________________

Reasons: ______________________________

____

____

5. Most class members want to have lunch together after the 9–11 A.M. final. You need to decide wher

Decision-making method recommended: ______________________________

Reasons: ______________________________

____

____

6. You work for a small company that wants to purchase a word processing/database software prograr that all employees will be using.

Decision-making method recommended: ______________________________

Reasons: ______________________________

____

____

7. You and your spouse are accepted into excellent but different graduate schools in different cities. You have two preschoolers and you both want to be together, but also want to participate in these programs (2–3 years).

Decision-making method recommended: ______________________________

Reasons: ______________________________

____

____

Part 2

Can you think of examples of times or places when you have used each of the types of decision making described in the text? Write at least one example of each.

consensus ______________________________

____

majority ______________________________

____

expert ______________________________

____

nority ______________________________

____

thority ______________________________

____

what situations are you most comfortable with each type of decision making?

nsensus ______________________________

ajority ______________________________

pert ______________________________

inority ______________________________

thority ______________________________

ecision-making method that I tend to gravitate toward: ______________________________

hy? ______________________________

____

____

ecision-making method I'm most comfortable with: ______________________________

ecision-making method I'm least comfortable with: ______________________________

NOTES ON THE NATURE OF GROUPS

NAME ________________________

[CH]APTER 8. ACTIVITY 5: EXPLORING THE WEB

1. Find the home page for the Center for Group Learning at *http://www.cgl.org/*. Who is the Center for Group Learning? What does CGL do?

____

____

____

2. Look at the various types of groups referred to on this Web site. List six different types of groups found here and not found in your text.

______________ ______________

______________ ______________

______________ ______________

3. List at least four different functions served by groups listed here:

GROUP NAME	MAJOR FUNCTION OR PURPOSE OF THE GROUP

4. Identify three groups that would best help members understand their strengths and weaknesses as communicators in groups. Explain why you think each of these groups would help participants understand themselves (as group members) better.

____

____

____

5. Choose four groups referred to in this Web site. After reading the description of each, predict whether each one is more likely to focus on task or social roles. Give the basis of your prediction.

GROUP NAME	PREDICTION: FOCUS ON TASK OR SOCIAL ROLES?	BASIS OF PREDICTION

6. Go to the "Other Group Resources Online" page which lists a number of group-related theories a practices. List four sources or sites that can enhance your understanding of groups.

____

____

____

____

NAME ______________________________

IAPTER 8 SELF TEST

ATCHING (KEY TERMS)

; 1

atch each term listed on the left with its correct definition from the column on the right.

_____ **1.** all-channel network
_____ **2.** chain network
_____ **3.** collectivistic orientation
_____ **4.** consensus
_____ **5.** dysfunctional role
_____ **6.** functional role
_____ **7.** gatekeeper
_____ **8.** group goals
_____ **9.** group
_____ **10.** growth group
_____ **11.** hidden agenda
_____ **12.** individual goals
_____ **13.** individualistic orientation
_____ **14.** learning group
_____ **15.** norms

a. network in which all parties have equal access to one another
b. person through whom information flows
c. small collection of individuals who interact over time to reach goals
d. shared values, beliefs, behaviors, and procedures that govern a group's operation
e. individual goals that group members are unwilling to reveal
f. group whose goal is to expand its members' knowledge about some outside topic
g. cultural orientation focusing on the group as a whole, rather than on concern by individuals for their own success
h. cultural orientation focusing on the value and welfare of individuals, as opposed to concern for the group as a whole
i. motives of separate group members that influence their behavior in the group
j. objectives that a group collectively seeks to accomplish
k. member role necessary for the group to accomplish its task-related goals
l. network in which information passes sequentially from one member to another
m. individual role of group member that inhibits the group's effectiveness
n. group whose goal is to help members learn more about themselves
o. agreement between group members about a decision

Set 2

_______ **16.** power distance

_______ **17.** problem-solving group

_______ **18.** procedural norm

_______ **19.** role fixation

_______ **20.** roles

_______ **21.** rules

_______ **22.** social group

_______ **23.** social norms

_______ **24.** social roles

_______ **25.** social goals

_______ **26.** sociogram

_______ **27.** task norms

_______ **28.** task orientation

_______ **29.** task roles

_______ **30.** task-related goals

_______ **31.** uncertainty avoidance

_______ **32.** wheel network

a. graphic representation of group interaction patterns
b. acting out a specific role whether or not the situation requires it
c. objectives related to accomplishing the group's stated purpose for existence
d. patterns of behaviors which help the group accomplish its goals
e. emotional roles concerned with maintaining harmonious personal relationships among group members (also called maintenance functions)
f. communication pattern in which a gatekeeper regulates the flow of information among other members
g. cultural tendency to seek stability and honc traditions instead of welcoming risk and change
h. degree to which members are willing to accept a difference in power and status among members
i. norm that describes rules for the group's operations
j. explicit, officially stated guideline that governs group functions and member behavior
k. task-related group whose goal is to resolve a mutual concern of its members
l. beliefs and behaviors that govern the relationship of group members to each other
m. beliefs and behaviors of a group that focus o how the job should be done
n. focus of the group on getting a job done
o. group whose goal is to meet the interaction needs of members
p. patterns of behavior expected of group members
q. motives of group members related to satisfying their interaction needs (inclusion, control, affection)

MULTIPLE CHOICE

Choose the BEST response from those listed.

1. Which is an essential part of the definition of a group?

a. individuals who interact verbally
b. individuals who interact face-to-face
c. individuals who interact over time
d. individuals who number at least five
e. all of the above

2. An investment group in which members join to understand and practice investments would be primarily a ________ group.

   a. learning
   b. growth
   c. problem-solving
   d. social
   e. none of the above

3. Group norms are best identified by

   a. observing the habits of members.
   b. reading the by-laws.
   c. noting how members are punished for behaviors.
   d. both a and b.
   e. both a and c.

4. A problem that occurs in groups with regard to roles is

   a. an important informal role is not filled.
   b. several people vie for a particular role.
   c. a member(s) acts out a certain role when the situation doesn't require it.
   d. All of the above can be problems in groups.
   e. None of these is a problem with regard to groups and roles.

5. You can be a more valuable group member if you

   a. look for missing roles; figure out what's not being done.
   b. fill or encourage others to fill missing roles.
   c. avoid role fixation when it is not helpful or needed.
   d. avoid dysfunctional roles.
   e. all of the above

6. One way to visually see who speaks to whom and how often is to construct a ________.

   a. sociogram
   b. role research diagram
   c. chain network
   d. collectivistic culture
   e. decision-making paradigm

7. Which network is described in this scenario? Jane stays at her desk and by her phone most of the workday. When others leave, they usually tell her. When Marcy is trying to reach Juan, but Juan is away from his desk, Marcy asks Jane to give Juan a message when he returns. Since Jane can see the other desks and is frequently asked to relay messages, she is performing the role of ________.

   a. chain network
   b. sociogram
   c. gatekeeper
   d. collectivistic orientation
   e. uncertainty avoider

8. Which network is represented in the following diagram?
   Driver——dispatcher——terminal manager——general manager

   a. wheel
   b. chain
   c. all-channel
   d. y-channel
   e. none of the above

9. In a wheel network, the gatekeeper

a. may distort messages to the detriment of the group.
b. may facilitate communication between members with strained relations.
c. is usually easily available and accessible to all members.
d. both b and c
e. all of the above

10. Which of the following is the major drawback of decision by consensus?

a. It's undemocratic.
b. Full participation in decision making decreases commitment to support the decision.
c. It is impossible to use expert opinion.
d. It takes a great deal of time.
e. Members don't get as involved emotionally as with other methods.

11. A group decision by minority often refers to a decision by

a. a group of rabble rousers.
b. committees.
c. a small group of external experts.
d. autocratic leaders.
e. none of the above

12. The best decision-making method depends on

a. the culture.
b. the importance of the decision.
c. the amount of time available.
d. characteristics of the group leader(s).
e. all of the above.

13. Usually members of individualistic cultures

a. are likely to produce and reward stars.
b. find consensus easy to achieve.
c. see their primary loyalty to groups.
d. are found predominantly in Asian and Latin American cultures.
e. are indirect.

14. U.S. cultures tend to

a. have a low power distance.
b. have high uncertainty avoidance.
c. be collectivistic.
d. have high social orientation.
e. none of the above

15. In a society with high power distance

a. leaders are not readily accepted and respected.
b. group members are not likely to feel they need a leader.
c. group members expect leaders to act like equals to all.
d. all of the above
e. none of the above

6. Societies with low uncertainty avoidance

a. are willing to take risks.
b. accept change readily.
c. see conflict as natural.
d. all of the above
e. none of the above

7. A virtual group generally has this advantage:

a. Status is leveled or less important among members.
b. speed and ease of meeting
c. reduced costs
d. all of the above
e. none of the above

ATCHING (ROLES)

atch the roles on the right with their types (A, B, C). You will need to use the letters more than once.

A. task role
B. social/maintenance role
C. dysfunctional role

_______ **1.** tension reliever
_______ **2.** information seeker
_______ **3.** cynic
_______ **4.** blocker
_______ **5.** gatekeeper
_______ **6.** orienter/summarizer
_______ **7.** elaborator/clarifier
_______ **8.** feeling expresser
_______ **9.** harmonizer
_______ **10.** dominator

UE/FALSE

rcle the T or F to indicate whether you believe the statement is true or false. If it is **true**, give a **reason** an **example**. If it is **false**, **explain** what would make it true.

F **1.** Any time you are surrounded by other people, you are part of at least one group.

____

____

F **2.** Majority-rule decisions are usually of higher quality than any other kind of decision.

____

____

F **3.** A decision by consensus means a vote of 51 percent or more.

____

____

T F **4.** Gatekeepers serve a vital communication function in a wheel network.

____

____

T F **5.** Role fixation occurs when a person enacts the same role in groups whether or not it is a needed or functional role for that context.

____

____

COMPLETION

Fill in each of the blanks with a word from the list provided. Choose the BEST word for each sentence. There are more words than you will use, but each word will be used only once.

formal roles	**social goals**	**norms**	**informal roles**
hidden agenda	**sociogram**		

1. Officially recognized and labeled behaviors, such as secretary, are known as ____________

2. Tasks or behaviors clearly operating but rarely acknowledged are called ____________

3. Important reasons for group membership, but reasons not always stated or recognized by member are called ____________.

4. An individual goal that is not made known to or shared with a group is a ____________

5. Unwritten rules that operate in groups are called ____________.

OTES ON THE NATURE OF GROUPS

CHAPTER 8. ANSWERS TO SELF TEST

MATCHING (KEY TERMS)

Set 1

1. a	**2.** l	**3.** g	**4.** o	**5.** m
6. k	**7.** b	**8.** j	**9.** c	**10.** n
11. e	**12.** i	**13.** h	**14.** f	**15.** d

Set 2

16. h	**17.** k	**18.** i	**19.** b	**20.** p
21. j	**22.** o	**23.** l	**24.** e	**25.** q
26. a	**27.** m	**28.** n	**29.** d	**30.** c
31. g	**32.** f			

MULTIPLE CHOICE

1. c	**2.** a	**3.** e	**4.** d	**5.** e
6. a	**7.** c	**8.** b	**9.** e	**10.** d
11. b	**12.** e	**13.** a	**14.** a	**15.** e
16. d	**17.** d			

MATCHING (ROLES)

1. B	**2.** A	**3.** C	**4.** C	**5.** B
6. A	**7.** A	**8.** B	**9.** B	**10.** C

TRUE/FALSE

1. F	**2.** F	**3.** F	**4.** T	**5.** T

COMPLETION

1. formal roles	**2.** informal roles	**3.** social goals	**4.** hidden agenda	**5.** norms

ELATED READING

'raternities and Rape on Campus," by Patricia Yancey Martin and Robert A. Hummer, *Gender & ociety* 3, no. 4 (December 1989): 457–573.

REVIEW:

roups can be powerful forces for good or for evil. What makes this article so pertinent to our chapter the nature of groups is its exploration of the norms in fraternities and how adherence to these norms ay perpetuate evil: the exploitation and rape of women. This investigation into the group dynamics of aternities shows that what results are often rules and roles which characterize patterns of interaction which coercion in sexual relations with women is normative. Authors Patricia Yancey Martin and bert A. Hummer contend that it is oversimplistic to conclude that fraternity members are more likely rape because of peer pressure. Rather, they assert that the more complex process of communication thin fraternities creates a view of women as commodities and thus creates a social context in which dividuals are more likely to rape. The article has a great deal of relevance to this chapter's discussion group dynamics and patterns of interaction; however, articles about violence toward others are never easy read and this one is no exception.

VIEW:

1. According to the authors of this article, how might membership in a fraternity shape a person's self-concept and perception of others?
2. What evidence do the authors present to substantiate their claim that "fraternities are a physical and sociocultural context that encourages the sexual coercion of women"?
3. Do you believe the authors would argue that the group norms shape the individuals or that the individuals shape the group norms? Explain your answer.
4. Explain how the transactional processes of communication and interaction shape our perception of and relationship with others, i.e., fraternity men and women.
5. Can you think of other groups in which cohesiveness may lead to similar violent problems? Should society play a role in reshaping or destroying these groups?

NOTES ON THE NATURE OF GROUPS

Chapter 9
Solving Problems in Groups

TER STUDYING THIS CHAPTER, YOU WILL BETTER UNDERSTAND:

1. The advantages of solving problems in groups.
2. The characteristics of several common discussion formats.
3. The six basic problem-solving steps in the rational problem-solving method.
4. The developmental stages in a problem-solving group.
5. The factors that contribute to group cohesiveness.
6. The factors that contribute to balanced participation in groups.
7. The various approaches to studying leadership.

TER STUDYING THIS CHAPTER, YOU WILL BE BETTER ABLE TO:

1. Use the problem-solving steps outlined in this chapter in a group task.
2. Suggest ways to build the cohesiveness and participation in a group.
3. Analyze the sources of leadership and power in a group.
4. Suggest the most effective leadership approach for a specific group task.
5. Identify the obstacles to effective functioning of a specific group and suggest more effective ways of communicating.

HAPTER 9 SKELETON OUTLINE

is outline can be a helpful study tool to assist you in seeing the order and sequence of the chapter and e relationship of ideas. Use it to take notes as you read and/or to add concepts presented in lecture.

I. PROBLEM SOLVING IN GROUPS: WHEN AND WHY

- **A.** Advantages of group problem solving
  - **1.** Resources
  - **2.** Accuracy
  - **3.** Commitment (participative decision making)
- **B.** When to use group problem solving
  - **1.** Job
  - **2.** Interdependence
  - **3.** Multiple solutions
  - **4.** Potential disagreement

I. TYPES OF PROBLEM-SOLVING FORMATS

- **A.** Buzz groups
- **B.** Problem census
- **C.** Focus group
- **D.** Parliamentary procedure
- **E.** Panel discussion
- **F.** Symposium
- **G.** Forum

III. APPROACHES AND STAGES IN PROBLEM SOLVING

- **A.** Structured problem-solving approach
  - **1.** Identify the problem/challenge
  - **2.** Analyze the problem
    - **a.** create probative questions
    - **b.** gather information
    - **c.** identify restraints/force field analysis
  - **3.** Develop creative solution
    - **a.** brainstorm
      - **(1)** no criticism
      - **(2)** freewheeling
      - **(3)** quantity
      - **(4)** combination
    - **b.** nominal group technique
      - **(1)** solo lists
      - **(2)** combining/no evaluation
      - **(3)** rank
      - **(4)** discussion
      - **(5)** decision
  - **4.** Evaluate solutions
    - **a.** desirability
    - **b.** implementation
    - **c.** disadvantages
  - **5.** Implementation
    - **a.** tasks
    - **b.** resources
    - **c.** responsibilities
    - **d.** emergencies
  - **6.** Follow up
    - **a.** periodic evaluation
    - **b.** revision as necessary
- **B.** Developmental stages in problem-solving groups
  - **1.** Orientation
  - **2.** Conflict
  - **3.** Emergence
  - **4.** Reinforcement

IV. MAINTAINING POSITIVE RELATIONSHIPS

- **A.** Basic skills
- **B.** Building cohesiveness
  - **1.** Cohesiveness and productivity
  - **2.** Boosting cohesiveness
    - **a.** shared/compatible goals
    - **b.** progress toward goals
    - **c.** shared norms and values
    - **d.** lack of perceived internal threats
    - **e.** interdependence
    - **f.** outside threat
    - **g.** mutual perceived attractiveness and friendship
    - **h.** shared group experiences

V. LEADERSHIP AND POWER IN GROUPS

- **A.** Power in groups
  - **1.** Types of power
    - **a.** legitimate power (position)/nominal leader
    - **b.** coercive power
    - **c.** reward power
    - **d.** expert power
    - **e.** referent power

2. Characteristics of power
   a. group-centered
   b. distributed
   c. not either–or

B. What makes leaders effective
   1. Trait analysis
   2. Leadership style
      a. communication style
         (1) authoritarian
         (2) democratic
         (3) laissez-faire
      b. leadership grid
         (1) production/task
         (2) concern for relationships
   3. Situational approaches
      a. changing circumstances
      b. group readiness

I. OVERCOMING DANGERS IN GROUP DISCUSSION

A. Information underload and overload
   1. Underload
   2. Overload

B. Unequal participation
   1. Advantages of participation
   2. Balance
   3. Encouraging participation
      a. size
      b. reinforcement
      c. tasks
      d. nominal group technique
   4. Discouraging unhelpful talk
      a. withhold reinforcement
      b. assert desire to hear from others
      c. challenge relevancy

C. Pressure to conform
   1. Recognizing groupthink
   2. Reducing groupthink

HAPTER 9 KEY TERMS

his list of key terms corresponds to those in boldface in your text. Use these lines to write the finition and/or an example of the word on the line next to it.

thoritarian leadership style ______________________________

____

ainstorming ______________________________

____

zz group ______________________________

____

coercive power ____________________

____

cohesiveness ____________________

____

conflict stage ____________________

____

democratic leadership style ____________________

____

emergence stage ____________________

____

expert power ____________________

____

focus group ____________________

____

force field analysis ____________________

____

forum ____________________

____

group think ____________________

____

information overload ____________________

____

information power ____________________

____

information underload ____________________

____

laissez-faire leadership style ____________________

____

ader ______________________________

____

adership ______________________________

____

gitimate power ______________________________

____

anagerial grid ______________________________

____

ominal leader ______________________________

____

ientation stage ______________________________

____

anel discussion ______________________________

____

arliamentary procedure ______________________________

____

articipative decision making ______________________________

____

oblem census ______________________________

____

ower ______________________________

____

robative question ______________________________

____

eferent power ______________________________

____

einforcement stage ______________________________

____

reward power ____________________

____

situational leadership ____________________

____

symposium ____________________

____

trait theories of leadership ____________________

____

NAME ______________________

HAPTER 9. ACTIVITY 1: TYPES OF POWER

RPOSE:

analyze types of power in different groups.

STRUCTIONS:

1. For each group that you list (or is already listed), consider the different types of power that various persons in the group have.
2. In the middle column, explain **your** relative amount of each type of power.
3. In the right column, describe who you believe has most of each type of power.

GROUP: ______________

DOES THE PERSON HAVE THIS TYPE OF POWER?	DISCUSS THE RELATIVE AMOUNT OF EACH TYPE OF POWER YOU HAVE.	WHO HAS THE MOST OF THIS TYPE OF POWER? WHY?
legitimate		
coercive		
reward		
expert		
referent		

GROUP: This Class

DOES THE PERSON HAVE THIS TYPE OF POWER?	DISCUSS THE RELATIVE AMOUNT OF EACH TYPE OF POWER YOU HAVE.	WHO HAS THE MOST OF THIS TYPE OF POWER? WHY?
legitimate		
coercive		
reward		
expert		
referent		

GROUP: ____________

DOES THE PERSON HAVE THIS TYPE OF POWER?	DISCUSS THE RELATIVE AMOUNT OF EACH TYPE OF POWER YOU HAVE.	WHO HAS THE MOST OF THIS TYPE OF POWER? WHY?
legitimate		
coercive		
reward		
expert		
referent		

GROUP: ____________________

DOES THE PERSON HAVE THIS TYPE OF POWER?	DISCUSS THE RELATIVE AMOUNT OF EACH TYPE OF POWER YOU HAVE.	WHO HAS THE MOST OF THIS TYPE OF POWER? WHY?
legitimate		
coercive		
reward		
expert		
referent		

GROUP: ____________________

DOES THE PERSON HAVE THIS TYPE OF POWER?	DISCUSS THE RELATIVE AMOUNT OF EACH TYPE OF POWER YOU HAVE.	WHO HAS THE MOST OF THIS TYPE OF POWER? WHY?
legitimate		
coercive		
reward		
expert		
referent		

NOTES ON SOLVING PROBLEMS IN GROUPS

NAME ______________________________

HAPTER 9. ACTIVITY 2: ENHANCING POWER IN GROUPS

RPOSE:

describe ways to enhance one's power in groups.

STRUCTIONS:

1. List four groups that you belong to.
2. Using Table 9-3: Methods for Acquiring Power in Small Groups from the text, list some specific ways that you could enhance your power in each of these groups.

ample:

roup I belong to: Investment group

hat I could do to enhance my power in that group and why: I could be sure that I can attend all eetings (visibility) and have my stock reports ready (demonstrate knowledge and follow group norms). hose who don't show up or never do their stock reports for the group lose credibility (legitimate thority). I could read and study more than our investment magazine and go to the extra workshops on ock analysis and then share that information with the group. (expert and information power) When it my turn to report on a stock, I can have copies for everyone or a clear overhead so that my ideas are early presented (referent power).

1. Group I belong to: ______________________________

   What I could do to enhance my power in that group and why: ______________________________

   ____

   ____

   ____

2. Group I belong to: ______________________________

   What I could do to enhance my power in that group and why: ______________________________

   ____

   ____

   ____

3. Group I belong to: ______________________________

   What I could do to enhance my power in that group and why: ______________________________

   ____

   ____

   ____

4. Group I belong to: ______________________________

What I could do to enhance my power in that group and why: ______________________________

____

____

____

NAME ______________________

APTER 9. ACTIVITY 3: COHESION IN GROUPS

RPOSE:

recognize ways of building cohesiveness in groups.

STRUCTIONS:

Read each of the items below. For each, decide which of the ways of building cohesion it most closely resembles. Some may be combinations of one or more.

Justify your answer.

shared/compatible goals | **progress toward goals** | **shared norms and values**

lack of perceived internal threats | **interdependence** | **outside threat**

mutual perceived attractiveness and friendship | **shared group experiences**

. A husband and wife planning a budget so they can purchase a home.

Greater cohesion could result from this because it is ______________________

____

However, cohesion wouldn't necessarily result because ______________________

____

. A group of students who band together to prevent tuition hikes threatened by the Board of Regents.

Greater cohesion could result from this because it is ______________________

____

However, cohesion wouldn't necessarily result because ______________________

____

. A group of cousins decides to go camping together.

Greater cohesion could result from this because it is ______________________

____

However, cohesion wouldn't necessarily result because ______________________

____

. A team went from all losses last year to 4–4 this year.

Greater cohesion could result from this because it is ______________________

____

However, cohesion wouldn't necessarily result because ______________________

____

5. A group of students knows that they all get the same grade on a project.

Greater cohesion could result from this because it is ______________________________

____

However, cohesion wouldn't necessarily result because ______________________________

____

6. A family goes on vacation together.

Greater cohesion could result from this because it is ______________________________

____

However, cohesion wouldn't necessarily result because ______________________________

____

7. A group of families in a neighborhood decides to clear a vacant lot to create a place for their children to play sports.

Greater cohesion could result from this because it is ______________________________

____

However, cohesion wouldn't necessarily result because ______________________________

____

NAME ____________________

[CH]APTER 9. ACTIVITY 4: GROUP COHESION CASE STUDY

[PU]RPOSE:

[To] apply information about group cohesion.

[IN]STRUCTIONS:

[Re]ad the case study below and answer the questions.

A group of business students decides to form an investment club to learn more about the stock market and investments, and to contribute small amounts of money ($10–$25) each month to be invested as a group. Mark and Maria, who came up with the idea, recruit some other students—Dan, Jana, and Jin-Sook. They realize the optimal number for an investment group is 12–15, so each agrees to recruit two or three more. A meeting time is set and the group discusses ways to get started: There are other organizations in town they can learn from as well as national organizations that they can affiliate with in order to use their materials, get their newsletters, etc.

[1]. What factors are already at work to promote cohesion? ____________________

____

____

____

[2]. At this point, if you were an advisor to the club, and you wanted to promote cohesiveness among group members, what four specific things would you recommend?

____

____

____

____

____

[Yo]ur turn: If you want more cohesiveness in a group you belong to, what can you do? Choose one group [an]d describe what you could do to promote cohesiveness.

____

____

____

____

____

____

NOTES ON SOLVING PROBLEMS IN GROUPS

NAME ____________________

APTER 9. ACTIVITY 5: EXPLORING THE WEB

TERNET RESOURCES: VIRTUAL TEAMS, GROUP COLLABORATION, FOCUS GROUPS

. **VIRTUAL TEAMS**
http://www.ascusc.org/jcmc/vol3/issue4/jarvenpaa.html

. Read the article "Communication and Trust in Global Virtual Teams" (June 1998), *Journal of Computer Mediated Communication.*

Summarize the thesis of that article:

____

____

____

Where is this journal published? ____________________

2. What are some communication behaviors that would promote trust in global virtual teams?

____

____

____

3. Use a search engine* with the term "virtual teams." How many Web pages do you find?

__________. How many courses can you find that offer communication skills for virtual teams?**

__________ Consulting firms that offer training for members of virtual teams? __________

Compare and contrast the training you find offered with the topics covered in this text:

____

____

____

Search engines: Yahoo!: *http://www.yahoo.com*
Alta Vista: *http://www.altavista.digital.com*

*A sample of virtual team training can be found at: *http://www.thevirtualteam.com*

II. **GROUP COLLABORATION**
http://www.labmed.umn.edu/~john/sgc/index.html

1. Read and list two key points from the introduction to "Small Group Collaboration on the Internet."

____

____

____

____

2. Go to the "Features Table." If your instructor or supervisor at work assigned you to a Web group today, which of the features listed are you familiar with?

Which would you need to become familiar with?

3. Go to the "Link Collections and Resources" site. Which resources appear to illustrate particular concepts from Chapter 9?

III. FOCUS GROUPS

1. Look at the list of over 50 articles on focus groups at *http://www.groupsplus.com/articles.htm.* What concerns appear with regard to using virtual or net-based focus groups?

2. Can you find an article that argues that net-based groups are NOT focus groups? Provide the author, title, name of publication, date, and the thesis of that article (if it is in full text) here:

NAME ______________________________

HAPTER 9 SELF TEST

ATCHING (KEY TERMS)

t 1

atch each term on the left with its correct definition from the column on the right.

_____ **1.** authoritarian leadership style
_____ **2.** brainstorming
_____ **3.** coercive power
_____ **4.** cohesiveness
_____ **5.** conflict stage
_____ **6.** democratic leadership style
_____ **7.** emergence stage
_____ **8.** expert power
_____ **9.** force field analysis
_____ **10.** forum
_____ **11.** group think
_____ **12.** information overload
_____ **13.** information power
_____ **14.** information underload
_____ **15.** laissez-faire leadership style
_____ **16.** leader

a. ability to influence others by virtue of the otherwise obscure information one possesses
b. style in which the designated leader uses legitimate, coercive, and reward power to dictate the group's actions
c. style in which the leader gives up formal leader role, transforming the group into a loose collection of individuals
d. totality of forces that causes members to feel themselves part of a group and makes them desire to remain in the group
e. ability to influence others by virtue of one's perceived superior skill
f. decline in efficiency that occurs when the rate or complexity of material is too great to manage
g. decline in efficiency that occurs when there is a shortage of information that is necessary to operate effectively
h. group's collective striving for unanimity that discourages realistic appraisals of alternatives to its chosen decision
i. a stage in problem solving when the group moves from conflict toward a single solution
j. method for generating ideas in groups by encouraging quantity and minimizing criticism
k. stage in problem-solving groups when members openly defend their positions and question those of others
l. ability to influence others by threat or imposition of unpleasant consequences
m. method of problem analysis that identifies the forces contributing to resolution of the problem and the forces that inhibit its resolution
n. style in which the nominal leader invites the group's participation in decision making
o. discussion format in which audience members are invited to add their comments to those of official discussants
p. person who heads a group

Set 2

_______ **17.** leadership

_______ **18.** legitimate power

_______ **19.** managerial grid

_______ **20.** nominal leader

_______ **21.** orientation stage

_______ **22.** panel discussion

_______ **23.** parliamentary procedure

_______ **24.** participative decision making

_______ **25.** power

_______ **26.** probative question

_______ **27.** referent power

_______ **28.** reinforcement stage

_______ **29.** reward power

_______ **30.** situational leadership

_______ **31.** symposium

_______ **32.** trait theories of leadership

_______ **33.** focus group

_______ **34.** buzz groups

a. theory that argues that the most effective leadership style varies according to leader–member relations, nominal leader's power, and task structure

b. person identified by title as the leader of a group

c. discussion format in which participants consider a topic conversationally, without formal procedural rules

d. ability to influence others by granting or promise of desirable consequences

e. two-dimensional model that describes various combinations of a leader's concern with task-related and relational goals

f. belief that it is possible to identify leaders b[y] personal traits (intelligence, appearance, sociability)

g. stage in problem-solving groups when members endorse the decision they have made

h. ability to influence others

i. problem-solving method in which specific rules govern the way issues may be discusse[d] and decisions made

j. subgroups (5–7) of a group too large for effective discussion which simultaneously discuss an issue

k. ability to influence a group owing to one's position in a group

l. stage in problem-solving groups when members become familiar with one another's positions and tentatively volunteer their own

m. ability to influence the behavior of others in a group

n. development of solutions with input by the people who will be affected

o. ability to influence others by virtue of the degree to which one is liked or respected

p. discussion format in which participants divide the topic to allow each to deliver in-depth information without interruptions

q. open question used to analyze a problem by encouraging exploratory thinking

r. groups formed to conduct market research

ULTIPLE CHOICE

oose the BEST response from those listed.

1. Groups are often effective in problem solving because they exhibit all of these except ________.

   a. greater resources
   b. greater accuracy
   c. greater commitment
   d. greater speed
   e. Groups have none of the above advantages.

2. Which question should be asked when trying to decide whether to use a group or an individual approach to problem solving?

   a. Is the job beyond the capacity of one person?
   b. Are the individual's tasks interdependent?
   c. Is there more than one decision or solutions?
   d. Is there potential for disagreement?
   e. All of the above are valid questions to ask when deciding whether to use a group or an individual approach.

3. Which type of problem-solving format is likely to use *Robert's Rules of Order*?

   a. parliamentary procedure
   b. panel discussion
   c. symposium
   d. forum
   e. Each of these typically follows *Robert's Rules.*

4. Which step is the first step in the structured problem-solving approach?

   a. Analyze the problem.
   b. Develop creative solutions.
   c. Implement the plan.
   d. Identify the problem.
   e. Evaluate the solutions.

5. Identifying specific tasks, determining necessary resources, defining individual responsibilities, and providing for emergencies are all part of which step of structured problem solving?

   a. Analyze the problem.
   b. Develop creative solutions.
   c. Implement the plan.
   d. Identify the problem.
   e. Evaluate the solutions.

6. Which of these is a probative question?

   a. Should we buy Macs or IBMs?
   b. What will we gain from new computer systems?
   c. Will the computers be paid for with cash or purchase orders?
   d. Resolved, that our company should purchase new computers.
   e. All of the above fall within the parameters of probative questions.

7. Probative questions and force field analysis are part of which step?

a. Analyze the problem.
b. Develop creative solutions.
c. Implement the plan.
d. Identify the problem.
e. Evaluate the solutions.

8. Brainstorming guidelines include all of the following **except**

a. No criticism.
b. Encourage freewheeling.
c. State your opposition clearly.
d. Seek quantity.
e. Combine and piggyback.

9. The difference between nominal groups and brainstorming is that

a. nominal groups allow members to work alone first.
b. brainstorming allows criticism; nominal group doesn't.
c. nominal groups seek quantity; brainstorming seeks quality.
d. brainstorming involves ranking ideas; nominal groups don't rank.
e. None of these is a difference.

10. Evaluating progress and revising the group's approach are part of which step?

a. Analyze the problem.
b. Follow up on the solution.
c. Implement the plan.
d. Identify the problem.
e. Evaluate the solutions.

11. Which is true of the reinforcement stage of group problem solving?

a. Members take strong positions and defend them.
b. Members are reluctant to take a stand.
c. Members approach consensus and back off dogmatic positions.
d. Members find reasons to endorse and support the decision.
e. None of these describes the reinforcement stage.

12. Such comments as "There are probably several ways we could approach this" and "I wonder wha would happen if we tried a new computer system" are typical of which stage?

a. orientation
b. conflict
c. emergence
d. reinforcement
e. These comments are typical of each stage.

13. There may be a lot of in-fighting within an organization, but when a perceived outside threat confronts the organization, the result is often

a. organizational ineffectiveness.
b. increased cohesiveness.
c. decreased cohesiveness.
d. contradictory feelings toward group leaders.
e. none of the above.

Which of these is true of power?

a. Power is conferred by a group; it is not an individual possession.
b. Power is distributed among group members; many members have different kinds of power.
c. Power is usually a matter of degree, not an all or nothing proposition.
d. All of these are true.
e. None of these is true.

You like getting invited to the boss's office often and getting to spend time sharing ideas with her. The fact that she can grant this time may represent a type of

a. coercive power.
b. reward power.
c. expert power.
d. referent power.
e. legitimate power.

Information overload

a. contributes to the quality of group decisions by having more information.
b. can be detrimental to a group.
c. is less and less a problem for groups who gather research well.
d. is usually less paralyzing to a group than information underload.
e. is unheard of in today's information age.

Leadership is often examined in terms of ________.

a. trait analysis
b. leadership style
c. situational variables
d. all of the above
e. none of the above

Leadership Grid looks at the relationship between a leader's concern for

a. referent and expert power issues.
b. democratic and authoritarian issues.
c. task and relational issues.
d. cohesiveness and interdependence.
e. none of the above

A leadership style that is laid back and not very involved is ________.

a. authoritarian
b. democratic
c. laissez-faire
d. trait analysis
e. none of the above

UE/FALSE

rcle the T or F to indicate whether you believe the statement is true or false. If it is **true**, give a **reason** an **example.** If it is **false**, **explain** what would make it true.

F **1.** In most cases, groups produce more and higher-quality solutions to problems than do individuals working alone.

____

____

T F **2.** In the emergence stage of problem solving, groups resolve their disagreements and solve their problem.

____

____

T F **3.** Groupthink refers to the ideal level of cohesion.

____

____

T F **4.** Participative decision making often produces members less likely to accept solutions and less committed to the decision than non-participative decision making.

____

____

T F **5.** If there is more than one decision or solution, it is best not to have a group tackle the problem; groups do better with problems that have a single answer.

____

____

COMPLETION

Fill in each of the blanks with a word from the list provided. Choose the BEST word for each sentence. There are more words than you will use, but each word will be used only once.

groupthink	**nominal group technique**	**information underload**	**interdependent**
laissez-faire	**power**	**force field analysis**	

1. Listing all of the items that would help and that would hinder a group in solving a problem is calle

______________________.

2. A technique that works to get many people's ideas out in group problem solving is called

______________________.

3. Excessive cohesiveness which often results in poor decision making is called ______________________

4. Group problem solving works best if the members have tasks that are ______________________.

5. In most groups, ______________________ is conferred by the group and distributed among members

NOTES ON SOLVING PROBLEMS IN GROUPS

CHAPTER 9 ANSWERS TO SELF TEST

MATCHING (KEY TERMS)

1. b	**2.** j	**3.** l	**4.** d	**5.** k
6. n	**7.** i	**8.** e	**9.** m	**10.** o
11. h	**12.** f	**13.** a	**14.** g	**15.** c
16. p				

Set 2

17. m (h)	**18.** k	**19.** e	**20.** b	**21.** l
22. c	**23.** i	**24.** n	**25.** h (m)	**26.** q
27. o	**28.** g	**29.** d	**30.** a	**31.** p
32. f	**33.** r	**34.** j		

MULTIPLE CHOICE

1. d	**2.** e	**3.** a	**4.** d	**5.** c
6. b	**7.** a	**8.** c	**9.** a	**10.** b
11. d	**12.** a	**13.** b	**14.** d	**15.** b
16. b	**17.** d	**18.** c	**19.** c	

TRUE/FALSE

1. T	**2.** T	**3.** F	**4.** F	**5.** F

COMPLETION

1. force field analysis	**2.** nominal group technique	**3.** groupthink
4. interdependence	**5.** power	

ELATED READING

welve Step Recovery and PTSD," by Patience Mason, *The Post-Traumatic Gazette* 1, no. 3 (Patience ess, P.O. Box 2757, High Springs, FL 32655). Available at *http://www.patiencepress.com/3rdIssue.htm.*

EVIEW:

ok at any city's listing of self-help groups and you will find Alcoholics Anonymous, Al-Anon (for family d friends of alcoholics), Overeater's Anonymous, and more. What these and many other self-help oups have in common is that they are Twelve-Step groups in which members recover from addiction trauma by using a model based on the Twelve Steps of Alcoholics Anonymous. Recently, PTSD (Post-aumatic Stress Disorder) groups have flourished to meet the needs of those who have endured and rvived war, rape, and natural disasters. In this article, Patience Mason, author of *Recovering from the ar: A Woman's Guide to Helping Your Vietnam Veteran, Your Family, and Yourself,* and editor of *The st-Traumatic Gazette,* a newsletter for friends, families, and therapists of trauma survivors, explains w Twelve-Step groups assist persons who want to recover. Groups are anonymous (using only first mes), fluid (different people attend from meeting to meeting, often with a "core" of regulars who tend at a particular time and place), and self-governing. If you are familiar with or practice a Twelve-ep program, you'll probably feel at home with this reading. If you are unfamiliar with Twelve-Step oups, you may want to read the Twelve Steps (remembering that different groups substitute propriate words for the word *alcohol*) before you read the article. As you read, strive to understand w Twelve-Step groups come to be so life changing and life saving for their members. Notice the unique ture of solving problems, distributing leadership, ensuring participation, and building cohesiveness in velve-Step groups.

EVIEW:

1. What does the author say is the correlation between admitting powerlessness (as in the first step) and empowerment?
2. Compare and contrast the structured problem-solving approach in the text and the Twelve-Step approach to a person's particular problem.
3. Underline the words *groups* and *meetings* throughout the article. How does the author impress upon readers the importance of meetings to recovery?
4. What contradiction does the author point out in court-mandated attendance in groups and the only requirement for group membership?
5. How does the author's description of leadership distribution and member participation compare and contrast with advice in the book?

NOTES ON SOLVING PROBLEMS IN GROUPS

Chapter 10
Choosing and Developing a Topic

FTER STUDYING THIS CHAPTER, YOU WILL BETTER UNDERSTAND:

1. The importance of choosing a topic and defining a clear speech purpose.
2. The difference between a general and a specific speech purpose.
3. The necessity of analyzing a speaking situation.
4. The importance of gathering information for a speech.

FTER STUDYING THIS CHAPTER, YOU WILL BE BETTER ABLE TO:

1. Choose an effective speech topic.
2. Formulate purpose statements that will help you develop that topic.
3. Analyze the key components of a speaking situation.
4. Gather information on your chosen topic from a variety of sources.

HAPTER 10 SKELETON OUTLINE

his outline can be a helpful study tool to assist you in seeing the order and sequence of the chapter and ie relationship of ideas. Use it to take notes as you read and/or to add concepts presented in lecture.

I. **CHOOSING A TOPIC**
   - A. Look for a topic early.
   - B. Choose a topic of interest to you.

II. **DEFINING A PURPOSE**
   - A. All communication is purposeful.
   - B. General purpose
     1. To entertain
     2. To inform
     3. To persuade
   - C. Specific purpose
     1. Purpose statement is receiver-oriented
     2. Purpose statement is specific
     3. Purpose statement is realistic
     4. Thesis statement
        - a. is the central idea of the speech
        - b. is delivered to the audience

II. **ANALYZING THE SPEAKING SITUATION**
   - A. Listeners (audience analysis and adapting to audience)
     1. Audience type
     2. Audience purpose
     3. Demographics

a. number of people
b. gender
c. age
d. group membership
e. other factors

4. Attitudes, beliefs, values
   a. attitudes
   b. beliefs
   c. values

B. Occasion
   1. Time
      a. time relates to other internal and external events
      b. time available
   2. Place
   3. Audience expectation

IV. **GATHERING INFORMATION**
   A. Internet research
      1. Search engines
      2. Evaluating Web sites
         a. credibility
         b. objectivity
         c. currency
   B. Library research
      1. Library catalog
      2. Reference works
      3. Periodicals
      4. Nonprint materials
      5. Databases
      6. Librarians
   C. Interviewing
   D. Personal observation
   E. Survey research

CHAPTER 10 KEY TERMS

This list of key terms corresponds to those in boldface in your text. Use these lines to write the definition and/or an example of the word on the line next to it.

attitude ______________________________

____

audience analysis ______________________________

____

belief ______________________________

____

database ______________________________

____

mographics

neral purpose

rpose statement

arch engine

arch string

ecific purpose

rvey research

esis statement

lue

NOTES ON CHOOSING AND DEVELOPING A TOPIC

NAME ______________________

[C]APTER 10. ACTIVITY 1: SPEECH TOPICS

[PU]RPOSE:

[To] explore interests and activities for possible speech topics.

[IN]STRUCTIONS:

[Fil]l in the blanks below with as much information as you can.

[Wh]at news stories in the past year have been of interest to you?

____

____

[W]hat are your favorite books?

____

____

[W]hat magazines do you read regularly?

____

____

[W]hat magazines interest you even if you do not find time to read them regularly?

____

____

[W]hat local events have fascinated you?

____

____

[W]hat makes your family interesting or unique?

____

____

[W]hat travel experiences have you had?

____

____

[W]hat activities do you participate in regularly?

____

____

What activities would you like to participate in but time or cost prohibit you?

What volunteer or service learning experiences have you had?

What jobs have you had?

List all the hobbies you have, even if you don't have as much time for them as you'd like.

What other hobbies have you pursued and been active in in the past?

What spiritual beliefs do you hold?

What beliefs do you hold with great intensity? [world population, antimaterialism, pro-life, pro/anti-military, environmentalist]

What activities do you regularly engage in? [Think of the mundane as well as the special: grocery shopping, car repairs, fitness center]

What awards have you received?

ıat probably makes you different from almost everyone in the class?

ıat common interests do you think you'd have with most everyone else in the class?

ıat experiences have you had as a teen or child that many people didn't have?

ıw, look over your lists. Which of these topics could become speech topics? List at least five potential ɔics.

TO INFORM	TO PERSUADE	TO ENTERTAIN

night be helpful to show your answers and your lists to a few classmates. Ask them to put a star side topics they would like to hear you speak on.

NOTES ON CHOOSING AND DEVELOPING A TOPIC

NAME ______________________________

CHAPTER 10. ACTIVITY 2: GENERAL PURPOSES, PURPOSE STATEMENTS, AND THESIS STATEMENTS

PURPOSE:

To ascertain the correlation between general purposes, purpose statements, and thesis statements.

INSTRUCTIONS:

1. For each purpose statement, tell the general purpose of the speech [inform, persuade, entertain].
2. Then construct a possible thesis for that speech.

1. After hearing my speech, audience members will be able to describe five characteristics of a flat tax.

   This purpose statement is probably for a speech to ______________________________.

   A possible thesis statement would be: ______________________________

   ____

2. After hearing my speech on the top four reasons to participate in karaoke singing, the audience will join me in a sing-along.

   This purpose statement is probably for a speech to ______________________________.

   A possible thesis statement would be: ______________________________

   ____

3. At the conclusion of my speech on the importance of corresponding with government officials, at least 15 audience members will pick up envelopes addressed to their congressional representatives and write each a letter.

   This purpose statement is probably for a speech to ______________________________.

   A possible thesis statement would be: ______________________________

   ____

4. After my presentation, audience members will understand four ways to be kind to the environment and be able to recite and explain the phrase: "Reuse, reduce, make do, go without."

   This purpose statement is probably for a speech to ______________________________.

   A possible thesis statement would be: ______________________________

   ____

5. Throughout my speech, I want my audience to laugh often and loudly and know that we Swedes have a sense of humor.

   This purpose statement is probably for a speech to ______________________________.

   A possible thesis statement would be: ______________________________

   ____

6. By the end of the week after hearing my speech, at least 50 percent of audience members will go to human resources and sign up for disability insurance.

This purpose statement is probably for a speech to ______________________________

A possible thesis statement would be: ______________________________

____

7. After hearing my speech on what a mill levy is, students will be able to define and explain the importance of the mill levy to their own education.

This purpose statement is probably for a speech to ______________________________

A possible thesis statement would be: ______________________________

____

8. After hearing my speech on the need for bone marrow donors to be registered in the national registry, all students will be able to describe the need and use for bone marrow and at least five will pick up registry forms and information.

This purpose statement is probably for a speech to ______________________________

A possible thesis statement would be: ______________________________

____

NAME ____________________

HAPTER 10. ACTIVITY 3: PURPOSE AND THESIS STATEMENTS

JRPOSE:

- identify well- and poorly written purpose statements

ART 1

ISTRUCTIONS:

1. For each of these purpose statements, tell whether it
   a = is a well-stated purpose statement
   b = is not receiver-oriented
   c = is not specific enough
   d = is not realistic

2. Rewrite any purpose statements that you marked b, c, or d, correcting the problem.

_____ **1.** At the conclusion of my speech, each member of the audience will purchase a package of Intergalactic Cheesecake.

_____ **2.** When I finish speaking, audience members will be better informed about Tae Bo workouts.

_____ **3.** At the end of my speech, the audience will know something about fat content of foods.

_____ **4.** When my presentation concludes, audience members will be able to cite five reasons for not allowing military recruiters in the high schools.

_____ **5.** At the conclusion of my speech, 50 percent of the audience given an exit survey will indicate that they plan to vote for my candidate.

_____ **6.** At the conclusion of my speech, a lot of the audience will prefer the idea of adoption rather than abortion.

_______ **7.** After my presentation, 60 percent of the students will be able to list at least three arguments for and three arguments against interracial adoption.

____

____

_______ **8.** By the time I finish speaking, audience members will be able to name and give significant information about the major ethnic groups of the former Yugoslavia.

____

____

PART 2

1. For each outline, write a possible thesis statement.

Sample:

Topic: Korean dance history

Major points I. Court dance forms
II. Religious dance forms
III. Folk dance forms

Possible thesis: Court dance, religious dance, and folk dance have different historical roots and represe distinct forms of Korean dance.

1. Topic: Martial arts training
Major points I. Mental benefits
II. Physical benefits
III. Safety benefits

Possible thesis: ____

____

2. Topic: Child care dilemmas
Major points I. Costs for parents
II. Trust and safety for child
III. Location and transportation

Possible thesis: ____

____

3. Topic: PC—Politically correct language
Major points I. Origins and intent
II. Objections and difficulties
III. The future of PC

Possible thesis: ____

____

4. Topic: Flat tax
   Major points
   I. Definition
   II. Advantages and disadvantages for government
   III. Advantages and disadvantages for three levels of taxpayers

   Possible thesis: ____

   ____

5. Topic: Investment strategies for college students
   Major points
   I. Stocks
   II. Bonds
   III. Mutual funds

   Possible thesis: ____

   ____

6. Topic: Taking your general electives at a community college
   Major points
   I. Cost
   II. Smaller classes, individual attention
   III. Transferability

   Possible thesis: ____

   ____

7. Topic: Public perception of the Clinton impeachment and trial
   Major points
   I. Personal history
   II. Party
   III. Gender

   Possible thesis: ____

   ____

8. Topic: Service learning on college campuses
   Major points
   I. Origin
   II. Benefits for students
   III. Benefits for community

   Possible thesis: ____

   ____

NOTES ON CHOOSING AND DEVELOPING A TOPIC

NAME ______________________________

GROUP) CHAPTER 10. ACTIVITY 4: DEMOGRAPHIC ANALYSIS

URPOSES:

1. To investigate the demographics of this class as part of an audience analysis.
2. To complete a demographic survey.

ISTRUCTIONS:

1. Complete the following information.
2. Share and tabulate the information as a class or turn in the pages to one group or individual who agrees to tabulate the information and report it to the whole class.
3. Use the "CLASS DEMOGRAPHICS: TALLY SHEET" at the end of this exercise to fill in the results. You will use this information again for an exercise in Chapter 11.

_____ Male _____ Female

ge category: _____ 18–24 _____ 25–30 _____ 31–40 _____ 41–50 _____ over 50

ear in school: _____ first year _____ sophomore _____ junior _____ senior

_____ already have a four-year degree, just taking the course

ajor: ____________________

thnic background: ____________________

roup membership:

ist groups that you belong to that are important to you, including, but not limited to, fraternities/ rorities, honor societies, religious groups, clubs, athletic groups

roup name/type ____________________ Group name/type ____________________

roup name/type ____________________ Group name/type ____________________

rimary reason for taking the class:

_____ It is required for my major or degree. _____ I needed something at this time.

_____ I needed it to prepare for/advance in my career. _____ It looked interesting.

_____ Other: ____

LASS DEMOGRAPHICS: TALLY SHEET

UMBERS: The class consists of a total of _______ students, _______ instructors, _______ TA's.

ENDER: The class consists of _______ males and _______ females.

GE: The class consists of the following number of students in each age category (put the number in ont of each category):

_____ 18–24 _____ 25–30 _____ 31–40 _____ 41–50 _____ over 50

YEAR IN SCHOOL: ______ first year ______ sophomore ______ junior ______ senior

______ already have a four-year degree, just taking the course

MAJOR: List major categories and lump those with few students together under "other."

Major: ______________________________ Number ______

Major: ______________________________ Number ______

Major: ______________________________ Number ______

Major: ______________________________ Number ______

Major: ______________________________ Number ______

Other: ______________________________ Number ______

ETHNIC BACKGROUND:

Ethnic background: ____________________ Number ______

Ethnic background: ____________________ Number ______

Ethnic background: ____________________ Number ______

Ethnic background: ____________________ Number ______

Ethnic background: ____________________ Number ______

GROUPS:

Group name/type ____________________ Number ______

Group name/type ____________________ Number ______

Group name/type ____________________ Number ______

Group name/type ____________________ Number ______

Group name/type ____________________ Number ______

Group name/type ____________________ Number ______

PRIMARY REASONS FOR TAKING THIS CLASS:

________ major/degree ________ time ________ career ________ interest ________ other

at general conclusions have you drawn about this audience?

____

____

____

____

____

____

w will these conclusions affect your selection and preparation of a speech topic?

____

____

____

____

NOTES ON CHOOSING AND DEVELOPING A TOPIC

NAME ____________________

APTER 10. ACTIVITY 5: EXPLORING THE WEB

MPARING SEARCH ENGINES AND EVALUATING WEB SITES

After reading the descriptions of the thirteen search engines found in Chapter 10 of the text, choose four of them. Select a potential speech topic, search, and compare the results.

pic: ____________________

SEARCH ENGINE USED	NUMBER OF HITS	VALUE OF SITES, REMARKS

Evaluating Web sites. Your text walks you through the process of evaluating Web sites. Choose two of the sites with different domain types (.com, .gov, .org, .edu) you found for a potential topic and answer the following for each site:

te 1: ____________________

EDIBILITY:

an you tell who wrote the page? If so, who? ____________________

re the authors' credentials listed? __________ If so, what are they?

____

____

o the credentials qualify them to write this document?

____

____

Is there a way to contact the page's authors? ____________________ If so, how? E-mail? Phone?

Address? ____

What institution publishes the document? ____

OBJECTIVITY:

Looking at the domain part of the address, identify whether the site is a commercial, a government, an organizational, or an educational site (usually identifiable by .com, .gov, .org, or .edu).

What type of site is it? ____

What biases may exist because of this? ____

Looking at the authors' credentials, what biases might exist? ____________________

____

CURRENCY:

Can you tell when the page was produced? ________ When? ______________

When was it last updated? ____________________

As you try the links from the page, how many or what percent work? ____________

How many or what percent are dead? ____________

Site 2: ____

CREDIBILITY:

Can you tell who wrote the page? If so, who? ____

Are the authors' credentials listed? __________ If so, what are they?

____

____

Do the credentials qualify them to write this document?

____

____

Is there a way to contact the page's authors? ____________________ If so, how? E-mail? Phone?

Address? ____

What institution publishes the document? ____

OBJECTIVITY:

Looking at the domain part of the address, identify whether the site is a commercial, a government, an organizational, or an educational site (usually identifiable by .com, .gov, .org, or .edu).

What type of site is it? ____

hat biases may exist because of this? ______

oking at the authors' credentials, what biases might exist? ______

______

RRENCY:

an you tell when the page was produced? ______ When? ______

hen was it last updated? ______

s you try the links from the page, how many or what percent work? ______

ow many or what percent are dead? ______

NOTES ON CHOOSING AND DEVELOPING A TOPIC

NAME ______________________________

IAPTER 10 SELF TEST

ATCHING (KEY TERMS)

atch each term listed on the left with its correct definition from the column on the right.

_____ **1.** attitude
_____ **2.** audience analysis
_____ **3.** belief
_____ **4.** database
_____ **5.** demographics
_____ **6.** general purpose
_____ **7.** purpose statement
_____ **8.** specific purpose
_____ **9.** survey research
_____ **10.** thesis statement
_____ **11.** value
_____ **12.** search engine
_____ **13.** search string

a. a technique for electronic searches in which several words are put together with precise linking words
b. a complete sentence describing the central idea of a speech
c. the precise effect that the speaker wants to have on an audience, expressed in the form of a purpose statement
d. a consideration of characteristics including the type, goals, demographics, beliefs, attitudes, and values of listeners
e. one of three basic ways a speaker seeks to affect an audience: to entertain, inform, or persuade
f. audience characteristics that can be analyzed statistically, such as age, gender, education, group membership, and so on
g. a deeply rooted belief about a concept's inherent worth
h. an underlying conviction about the truth of an idea, often based on cultural training
i. information gathering in which the responses of a sample of a population are collected to disclose information about the larger group
j. a computerized collection of information that can be searched in a variety of ways to locate information
k. an electronic library catalog or index
l. a complete sentence that describes precisely what a speaker wants to accomplish
m. predisposition to respond to an idea, a person, or a thing favorably or unfavorably

MULTIPLE CHOICE

Choose the BEST response from those listed.

1. When choosing a topic for a speech, your text suggests it is best to

a. choose a topic about which you know nothing so your topic will be fresh.
b. choose a topic which you are not really interested in so you empathize with the audience and develop their interest.
c. delay your choice as long as possible so that you spend as much time as you can searching for a good topic.
d. choose a topic that interests you so you can make it interesting for others.
e. choose a topic you've already written an essay on so you can just present the essay.

2. Which is NOT a general purpose?

   a. to inform
   b. to persuade
   c. to review
   d. to entertain
   e. All are general purposes.

3. Which is true of a general speech purpose?

   a. Most speeches have ONLY ONE purpose.
   b. Purposes are interrelated and cumulative.
   c. The general purpose is expressed in a purpose statement.
   d. The general purpose is the same as a specific purpose.
   e. All of the above are true.

4. Which is an effective purpose statement?

   a. The purpose of my speech is to inform.
   b. After my speech, the audience will be able to list four reasons why young people join gangs.
   c. My purpose is to inform you about crime and persuade you to stay out of gangs.
   d. The purpose is to inform the audience about crime.
   e. I want to tell my audience about the purpose of the Douglas Crime Bill.

5. An effective purpose statement

   a. is realistic.
   b. is specific.
   c. is receiver-oriented.
   d. does all of the above.
   e. does none of the above.

6. Which is a thesis statement?

   a. Changing the way we fund campaigns will benefit candidates and voters.
   b. Adapting to a new CEO is like changing a tire.
   c. College students work hard.
   d. After my speech the officers (audience) will be able to distinguish a bribery overture from innocent small talk.
   e. I want to tell the audience about radial keratotomy surgery.

7. Passersby, captives, and volunteers are types of

   a. audiences.
   b. general purposes.
   c. speakers.
   d. occasions.
   e. specific purposes.

8. With regard to audience purpose, it is generally reasonable to say

   a. all members are there for the same purpose.
   b. there may be a variety of purposes for listening within an audience.
   c. gender is generally the best predictor of purpose.
   d. audience demographics have no correlation to audience purpose.
   e. none of these is true.

Which of these is not a demographic factor?

a. number of people
b. age
c. speech purpose
d. sex
e. group membership

A predisposition to respond to something in a favorable or unfavorable way is a/an ________.

a. belief
b. demographic
c. attitude
d. purpose
e. value

One author referred to in your text cited five values shared by most Americans. Which is **not** one of them?

a. citizenship
b. materialism
c. tolerance
d. individualism
e. work ethic

2. When considering time as part of an audience analysis, a speaker should include which of these?

a. Consider how much time you have been allotted or assigned.
b. Consider what world or local events might be occurring the same day as your speech.
c. Consider whether it is morning or after lunch, the beginning or end of some shared segment of time (semester, retreat), or a calendar holiday.
d. All of these are valid time considerations.
e. None of these is what is meant by considering time as part of audience analysis.

3. "The group I will be speaking to is composed of mostly Euroamerican, middle-class males who have been successful in business. Most are middle-aged and college-educated." Those statements are typical of statements from

a. a specific purpose.
b. a general purpose.
c. an audience analysis.
d. a speaker analysis.
e. a thesis statement.

14. Which of these could be used for research for a speech?

a. database
b. search engine
c. Web site
d. periodical
e. all of the above

15. Reviewing your interests is a good step to take when

a. analyzing the audience.
b. analyzing the speaking situation.
c. choosing a topic.
d. organizing your speech.
e. It is not helpful for any of these tasks.

TRUE/FALSE

Circle the T or F to indicate whether you believe the statement is true or false. If it is **true,** give a **reas** or an **example**. If it is **false, explain** what would make it true.

T F **1.** Personal experience should never be used for research for a speech.

____

____

T F **2.** If your speech is very good, there is no need to consider what other speakers may say before you or what recent events the audience may be concerned with.

____

____

T F **3.** Research for a speech is not limited to books and articles; it may include several nonprint sources.

____

____

T F **4.** A good purpose statement will be oriented toward the listeners.

____

____

T F **5.** A thesis statement is purposefully vague.

____

____

COMPLETION

Fill in each of the blanks with a word from the list provided. Choose the BEST word for each sentence. There are more words than you will use, but each word will be used only once.

actions	**persuade**	**time**	**attitudes**
entertain	**interview**	**audience**	**analyze**

1. You can often make an inference about audience __________________ by identifying their beliefs and values.

2. In preparing a speech, the speaker should analyze the __________________ and the occasion.

3. __________________, place, and audience expectation are three key elements of audience analysis.

4. A nonprint research source for a speech is a/an __________________.

5. An after-dinner speech probably has as its primary purpose to __________________.

OTES ON CHOOSING AND DEVELOPING A TOPIC

CHAPTER 10 ANSWERS TO SELF TEST

MATCHING (KEY TERMS)

1. m	**2.** d	**3.** h	**4.** j	**5.** f
6. e	**7.** l	**8.** c	**9.** i	**10.** b
11. g	**12.** k	**13.** a		

MULTIPLE CHOICE

1. d	**2.** c	**3.** b	**4.** b	**5.** d
6. a	**7.** a	**8.** b	**9.** c	**10.** c
11. b	**12.** d	**13.** c	**14.** e	**15.** c

TRUE/FALSE

1. F	**2.** F	**3.** T	**4.** T	**5.** F

COMPLETION

1. attitude	**2.** audience	**3.** time	**4.** interview	**5.** entertain

ELATED READING

:ecilia Fire Thunder: She Inspires Her People," by Ann Davis, *New Directions for Women* anuary/February 1991), pp. 12–13.

REVIEW:

this article, author Ann Davis introduces us to Cecilia Fire Thunder, a Sioux who speaks frequently to ative and Non-native audiences alike. Chapter 10 depicts the importance of choosing topics well suited you, of defining your purpose and thesis, and of analyzing the speaking situation, including the dience, the occasion, and yourself. As you read, note how Cecilia Fire Thunder creates and adapts her essage and her visual aids to her audience. Notice how she handles the dialectical tension between eaking out on what she feels needs to be said and doing so in such a way that her intended audience ntinues to listen to her. She experiences firsthand the criticism of those who believe her choice of pics would better be left alone.

EVIEW:

1. What statements by Cecilia Fire Thunder indicate a clear understanding of herself as a speaker?
2. What statements show a keen awareness of the attitudes, beliefs, and values of the audience?
3. How are the problems of alcoholism, domestic violence, and child abuse addressed? What was the role of communication, and public speaking in particular, in addressing these issues?
4. Describe how Fire Thunder's unique combination of purposes, feelings, knowledge, and interests gives her particular competencies to speak out.

NOTES ON CHOOSING AND DEVELOPING A TOPIC

Chapter 11
Organization and Support

FTER STUDYING THIS CHAPTER, YOU WILL BETTER UNDERSTAND:

1. The importance of clear speech organization.
2. The basic structure of a speech.
3. The steps involved in organizing the body of a speech.
4. The importance of effective introductions, conclusions, and transitions.
5. The functions and types of supporting materials, including visual aids.

FTER STUDYING THIS CHAPTER, YOU WILL BE BETTER ABLE TO:

1. Construct an effective speech outline, using the organizing principles described in this chapter.
2. Develop effective introductions, conclusions, and transitions.
3. Choose verbal supporting material for a speech to make your points clear, interesting, memorable, and convincing.
4. Choose appropriate visual aids for presentation.

HAPTER 11 SKELETON OUTLINE

his outline can be a helpful study tool to assist you in seeing the order and sequence of the chapter and e relationship of ideas. Use it to take notes as you read and/or to add concepts presented in lecture.

I. STRUCTURING THE SPEECH

- **A.** Types of outlines
  - **1.** Working outlines
  - **2.** Formal outlines
  - **3.** Speaking notes

II. PRINCIPLES OF OUTLINING

- **A.** Symbols
- **B.** Format
- **C.** Rule of division
- **D.** Rule of parallel wording

III. ORGANIZING IN LOGICAL ORDER

- **A.** Time patterns
- **B.** Space patterns
- **C.** Topic patterns
- **D.** Problem–solution patterns
- **E.** Cause–effect patterns
- **F.** Motivated sequence
  - **1.** Attention
  - **2.** Need

3. Satisfaction
4. Visualization
5. Action

G. Climax patterns

IV. USING TRANSITIONS

A. Internal previews

B. Internal reviews

V. BEGINNING AND ENDING THE SPEECH

A. Introduction
1. Capture attention
   a. refer to audience
   b. refer to occasion
   c. refer to relationship of audience and subject
   d. refer to something familiar
   e. cite startling fact or opinion
   f. ask a question
   g. tell an anecdote
   h. use a quotation
   i. tell a joke
2. Preview main points
3. Set the mood and tone
4. Demonstrate topic's importance

B. Conclusion
1. Functions
   a. review thesis (summary statement)
   b. ensure memory
2. Mistakes to avoid
   a. ending abruptly
   b. rambling
   c. introducing new points
   d. apologizing

VI. SUPPORTING MATERIAL

A. Functions
1. To clarify
2. To add interest
3. To make memorable
4. To prove

B. Types
1. Definitions
2. Examples
   a. factual
   b. hypothetical
3. Statistics
4. Analogies/comparison–contrast
5. Anecdotes
6. Quotation/testimony

C. Styles
1. Narration
2. Citation

VII. USING VISUAL AIDS

A. Purposes
1. How things look
2. How things work

   3. How things relate
   4. Clarity
- **B.** Types
   1. Objects and models
   2. Diagrams
   3. Word and number charts
   4. Pie charts
   5. Bar and column charts
   6. Line charts
- **C.** Media for presentation
   1. Chalkboard, white board, polymer marking surface
   2. Flip pad/poster board
   3. Handout
   4. Projector
   5. Other electronic media
- **D.** Rules for use
   1. Simplicity
   2. Size
   3. Attractiveness
   4. Appropriateness
   5. Reliability

CHAPTER 11 KEY TERMS

This list of key terms corresponds to those in boldface in your text. Use these lines to write the definition and/or an example of the word on the line next to it.

analogy ______________________________

____

anecdote ______________________________

____

bar chart ______________________________

____

basic speech structure ______________________________

____

cause–effect pattern ______________________________

____

citation ______________________________

____

climax pattern ______________________________

____

column chart ____

conclusion

diagram

example

formal outline

hypothetical example

introduction

line chart

model

narration

number chart

pie chart

problem–solution pattern

space pattern

;atistics ______________________________

____

ɜstimony ______________________________

____

.me pattern ______________________________

____

ɔpic pattern ______________________________

____

ransition ______________________________

____

isual aid ______________________________

____

ord chart ______________________________

____

orking outline ______________________________

____

NOTES ON ORGANIZATION AND SUPPORT

NAME ____________________

HAPTER 11. ACTIVITY 1: PARALLEL WORDING AND FORMAT

JRPOSE:

› practice parallel wording for outlines.

ISTRUCTIONS:

›r each of the following main points of outlines, rewrite them in a parallel fashion.

:ample:

ıe family of the 21st century will probably have experienced divorce.

venty-first–century families may have children through increased fertility technology.

ore families in the next century will be interracial.

written in Parallel Form:

venty-first-century families will likely be divided by divorce.

venty-first-century families will likely be expanded by fertility technology.

venty-first-century families will likely be enriched by interracial connections.

1. You should never leave your doors unlocked.
   Be sure to carry a flashlight and flares.
   Don't ever travel without adequate pre-trip maintenance to your vehicle.

   Rewritten in parallel form:

   ____

   ____

   ____

2. Future goals for humankind should be to end warfare and violence.
   If we are to survive the next century, we need to understand and build community.
   The environment is the greatest concern of the next century.

   Rewritten in parallel form:

   ____

   ____

   ____

3. Education must include fluency in several languages.
   Without computer skills, there is no point in other education.
   The whole point of education is to learn how to learn.

   Rewritten in parallel form:

   ____

   ____

   ____

OUTLINING PRACTICE. Read the sentences below and figure out which is the thesis statement. Write that on the line indicated. Now, put the remaining sentences in correct outline form.

Community agencies gain stronger connections with college resources and personnel.
Service Learning benefits faculty and classrooms.
Service Learning programs benefit students, the community, and faculty.
Students discover the correleation between theory and practice.
Service Learning benefits students academically and personally.
Students return to the classroom and provide faculty and other students with real-life examples.
Service Learning benefits community agencies.
Students bring enthusiasm and talents and hours of service to agencies.
Faculty become aware of new areas for research and societal connections to academic areas.
Students develop networks for personal interests and possible career choices.

Thesis statement: ____

____

____

____

____

____

____

____

____

____

____

NAME ______________________________

IAPTER 11. ACTIVITY 2: LOGICAL ORDER

RPOSE:

practice various outline forms.

STRUCTIONS:

ing "my life" (or pick someone else's life that you are familiar with, either a public figure or other lividual you are familiar with) as the topic, show a thesis statement and three or four main points for ch of the following types of outlines.

ample:

ACE PATTERN

esis: I've lived in several parts of the country, and learned something from each one.

I. In Texas, I learned the electric slide and the secret of barbecue.

I. In Maine, I learned to sail and appreciate sunrises.

I. In Minnesota, I learned to make leftsa and dance the polka.

IE PATTERN

esis: ______________________________

____

. ______________________________

. ______________________________

I. ______________________________

ACE PATTERN

hesis: ______________________________

____

I. ______________________________

I. ______________________________

I. ______________________________

PIC PATTERN

hesis: ______________________________

____

I. ______________________________

I. ______________________________

II. ______________________________

Choose your city, your university, or another city or university you are familiar with and show a thesis and main points for these types of outlines.

PROBLEM–SOLUTION

Thesis: ______________________________

____

I. ______________________________

II. ______________________________

III. ______________________________

CAUSE–EFFECT

Thesis: ______________________________

____

I. ______________________________

II. ______________________________

III. ______________________________

NAME ______________________________

'HAPTER 11. ACTIVITY 3: INTRODUCTIONS

'URPOSE:

'o identify various types of introductory techniques.

NSTRUCTIONS:

1. Read each of the introductory statements below.
2. For each, identify which type of introductory technique is used.
3. Write those words on the line. If you think the statement is a combination of two techniques, write both on the line.

'echniques:

Refer to the audience

Refer to the relationship between audience and subject

Refer to something familiar to the audience

Cite a startling fact or opinion

Ask a question

Tell an anecdote

Use a quotation

Tell a joke

1. "If I were an American and you were an American audience, I would probably begin my speech with a joke. If I were Japanese speaking to a Japanese audience, I would probably begin with an apology. Since I am neither American nor Japanese, I will begin with an apology for not telling a joke."—R. Moran

   Introductory technique: ______________________________

2. Today is a very special day in the lives of these young people seated before us. It is a day they will always refer to as their graduation day.

   Introductory technique: ______________________________

3. William Butler Yeats said, "Education is not filling a bucket but lighting a fire." These words give us much to ponder tonight as we debate the future of this educational institution.

   Introductory technique: ______________________________

4. The number one fear of most Americans is public speaking! That's right. In surveys of U.S. Americans, the fear of public speaking even ranked above the fear of dying.

   Introductory technique: ______________________________

5. As I begin my after-dinner speech tonight, I'd like to know how many of you know the fat content or number of grams of fat of the meal we just ate together?

   Introductory technique: ______________________________

NOTES ON ORGANIZATION AND SUPPORT

NAME ______________________________

IAPTER 11. ACTIVITY 4: SUPPORTING MATERIALS

IRPOSE:

identify and understand types of supporting materials.

RT 1

ISTRUCTIONS:

atch each selection with its correct label:

amples	descriptions	definitions	analogies
ecdotes	statistics		

______________ **1.** $35 provides clean water for 40 refugees. $100 provides antibiotics for 40 wounded children. $500 provides 1,000 people with emergency sanitation materials.

______________ **2.** Sleeping sickness is transmitted from person to person by the tsetse fly with devastating effects. Once infected, victims become feverish and weak and their thinking is distorted. They are literally overcome by sleep, losing all control over sleeping and waking cycles. Eventually, sleep turns into coma, coma to death.

______________ **3.** Doctors Without Borders responds to natural disasters. In November 1995, North Korea was hit with severe floods followed closely by subzero weather. Doctors Without Borders provided emergency medical supplies and care, supplementary nutrition, and health kits. In Pakistan and Bangladesh, similar assistance was provided.

______________ **4.** Sleeping sickness is like a silent killer.

______________ **5.** When the Blizzard of '96 struck the east coast, Dr. Evan Lee couldn't get to work at his Boston hospital. Not because of the snow—but because he was in Uganda, eradicating the deadly "sleeping sickness" as a Doctors Without Borders volunteer.

______________ **6.** Yellow fever is a lethal, mosquito-borne virus that causes death by massive bleeding from the eyes, nose, mouth, bladder, and other organs.

nformation from the Doctors Without Borders/Medecins Sans Frontieres Newsletter, March 1996.]

ART 2

or each of the following, determine what types of supporting material you would need and give reasons r your choices.

1. A speech to convince classmates to give to your favorite charity.

Types of supporting material I'd want to use: ______________________________

____

Reasons: ______________________________________

____

2. A speech to explain differences between Van Gogh's and Rembrandt's styles.

Types of supporting material I'd want to use: ______________________________

____

Reasons: ______________________________________

____

3. A speech which explains the advantages and disadvantages of using computers to create sets for films rather than constructing life-size sets.

Types of supporting material I'd want to use: ______________________________

Reasons: ______________________________________

NAME ______________________________

HAPTER 11. ACTIVITY 5: VISUALS

JRPOSE:

› practice constructing various types of visuals.

ISTRUCTIONS:

1. Use the information gathered in the demographic survey in Chapter 10, Activity 4 in this manual.
2. Take some of that information and create each of the following in a way that would be useful for a visual aid for a speech.

ake a bar chart to show the number of males and females.

Iake a column chart to show the number of students in each age category.

Make either a bar or column chart to show the number of students classified as first year, sophomore, etc.

Make a word chart to show the majors of students in the class.

Make a pie chart showing the primary reasons students take this class.

Use the following information to create a line graph.

Announced layoffs from major corporations (*Newsweek,* February 26, 1996):

AT&T 1/96: 40,000
Boeing 2/93: 28,000
Chemical/Chase Manhattan 8/95: 12,000
Delta Air Lines 4/94: 15,000
Digital Equipment 5/94: 20,000
GTE 1/94: 17,000
IBM 7/93: 60,000
Nynex 1/94: 16,800
Sears 1/93: 50,000

Thousands of people laid off:

1992 199

REATE YOUR OWN VISUAL

u are writing a speech to convince the audience that every dollar counts when donated to Doctors ithout Borders *(www.doctorswithoutborders.org),* decide on the best type of visual to convey the llowing information. Use your computer if possible (or sketch below) to create the best visual.

35 supplies a basic suture kit to repair minor shrapnel wounds
70 provides clean water for 85 refugees a day
100 provides antibiotics to treat nearly 40 wounded children
250 supplies 175 days of high-protein food for malnourished children
500 brings emergency medical supplies to aid 2,500 refugees for a month

NOTES ON ORGANIZATION AND SUPPORT

NAME ______________________________

[CH]APTER 11. ACTIVITY 6: EXPLORING THE WEB

[US]ING THE WEB TO ANALYZE SUPPORTING MATERIAL

[Us]ing one or more speeches found at the Speech and Transcript Center at *http://gwis2.circ.gwu.edu/ [~g]price/speech.htm,* find at least two examples of each type of supporting material listed below. Note the [spe]aker and write the example on the lines provided.

[1]. Definitions: ______________________________

____

____

____

____

____

[2]. Examples: ______________________________

____

____

____

____

____

3. Analogies: ______________________________

____

____

____

____

____

4. Anecdotes: ______________________________

____

____

____

____

____

5. Now, use one of these sites to find statistics for a speech to inform the audience about the increasing diversity of the United States. Then write several sentences to show how you would translate the statistics into clear lines of a speech.

   Fedstats: *www.fedstats.gov*
   Census Bureau: *www.census.gov*
   Bureau of Labor Statistics: *stats.bls.gov/blsome.html*

   ____

   ____

   ____

6. Choose a possible topic for an informative speech. (use the topic you are actually giving a speech in this class if possible). Find two quotations that could be used for support or for an introduction a conclusion using Bartlett's Web site at *http://www.columbia.edu/acis/bartleby/bartlett.* Write th quotations and authors below.

   Topic: ____

   Quotations: ____

   ____

   ____

   ____

   ____

NAME ________________________________

APTER 11 SELF TEST

TCHING I (KEY TERMS)

tch each term listed on the left with its correct definition from the column on the right.

_____ 1. analogy

_____ 2. anecdote

_____ 3. bar chart

_____ 4. basic speech structure

_____ 5. cause–effect pattern

_____ 6. citation

_____ 7. climax pattern

_____ 8. column chart

_____ 9. conclusion

_____ 10. diagram

_____ 11. example

_____ 12. formal outline

_____ 13. hypothetical example

_____ 14. introduction

_____ 15. line chart

a. visual aid that compares two or more values by showing them as elongated vertical rectangles

b. example that asks an audience to imagine an object or event

c. visual aid consisting of a grid that maps out the direction of a trend by plotting a series of points

d. organizing plan for a speech that builds ideas to the point of maximum interest or tension

e. consistent format and set of symbols used to identify the structure of ideas

f. visual aid that compares two or more values by showing them as elongated horizontal rectangles

g. a specific case used to demonstrate a general idea

h. first structural unit of a speech which gets attention and previews main points

i. brief statement of supporting material in a speech

j. extended comparison that can be used as supporting material in a speech

k. a division of a speech into introduction, body, and conclusion

l. speech organizing plan that demonstrates how one or more events result in another event

m. line drawing that shows important components of an object

n. a brief story used to illustrate or support a point in a speech

o. final structural unit of a speech which reviews main points and motivates audience to act or remember

MATCHING II

_______ **16.** model
_______ **17.** narration
_______ **18.** working outline
_______ **19.** pie chart
_______ **20.** problem–solution pattern
_______ **21.** transition
_______ **22.** space pattern
_______ **23.** statistics
_______ **24.** testimony
_______ **25.** time pattern
_______ **26.** topic pattern
_______ **27.** visual aid

a. organizational pattern that describes an unsatisfactory state of affairs and then proposes a plan to remedy the problem
b. visual aid that divides a circle into wedges, representing percentages of the whole
c. a tool used to build your speech, showing your constantly changing arrangement of ideas
d. pattern of speech organization based on location
e. scaled representations of an object
f. presentation of speech support material as story
g. supporting material that proves or illustrates a point by citing an authoritative source
h. pattern of speech organization according to chronology
i. phrase that connects ideas in a speech by showing how one relates to the other
j. numbers arranged to show how a fact or principle is true for a large number of cases
k. organizing scheme that arranges points according to logical types or categories
l. a device to show how things look, relate, or work

MULTIPLE CHOICE

Choose the BEST response from those listed.

1. Which is a correct use of formal outline form symbols?

a.
- I.
  - A.
  - B.
- II.
  - A.
  - B.
    - a.
    - b.

b.
- A.
  - I.
  - II.
- B.
  - 1.
- C.
  - 1.
  - 2.

c.
- I.
  - a.
  - b.
- II.
  - a.
  - b.
- III.

d.
- I.
  - A.
    - 1.
    - 2.
  - B.
- II.
  - A.
  - B.

2. Healthy foods **need not be** tasteless.
Healthy foods **need not be** dull.
Healthy foods **need not be** costly.

The **boldfaced parts** of the above sentences represent the rule of _________.
a. division
b. parallel wording
c. logical order
d. chronological order
e. none of the above

3. The climactic pattern tends to

   a. move the audience to action.
   b. overcome the effects of an anticlimactic introduction.
   c. create suspense.
   d. create the illusion of being ethical.
   e. all of the above

4. Which is NOT a function of transitions?

   a. support and explain main points
   b. show how the introduction correlates to the body
   c. make the correlation of the main point to the subpoint
   d. show how the supporting materials relate to the points they support
   e. make the connection of the main points to each other clear

5. Which of these is a transition?

   a. Tonight, I'd like to talk with you about the crime rate in our city.
   b. In addition to a rise in property crime, we're also seeing an increase in violent crime.
   c. Crime can be defined as any act which violates an established law.
   d. Imagine yourself coming home and finding your apartment ransacked, your computer and VCR gone, and your windows smashed.
   e. So, follow these guidelines and protect yourself from crime!

6. Which of these is NOT an appropriate way to begin a speech?

   a. refer to the audience
   b. refer to the occasion
   c. cite a startling fact or opinion
   d. ask a question
   e. apologize for any upcoming errors

7. Which of these is NOT an appropriate concluding technique?

   a. use strong, memorable words
   b. restate the thesis
   c. review main points
   d. relate the subpoints to the main points
   e. All of these are a part of the conclusion.

8. According to your text, which of these is NOT a function of supporting material?

   a. to present new points
   b. to clarify points
   c. to make points interesting
   d. to make points memorable
   e. to prove a point

9. This quotation relates to the skill it takes to create which part of a speech? "A speech is like a love affair. Any fool can start it, but to end it requires considerable skill."—Lord Mancroft

   a. transition
   b. introduction
   c. body
   d. conclusion
   e. support material

10. The boldfaced part of Henry David Thoreau's remark, "The basic trick is to choose the right words and put them in the **right order**," relates most closely to the purpose of ________.

   a. organizational patterns
   b. supporting material
   c. introductions
   d. conclusions
   e. definitions

11. The best way to write effective transitions is to

   a. tell an anecdote.
   b. use a quotation.
   c. tell a joke.
   d. have good supporting material for the transition.
   e. show a connection or correlation between parts.

12. Which of these is NOT a type of supporting material?

   a. examples
   b. definitions
   c. statistics
   d. quotations
   e. organization

13. Which of these is an operational definition of a mother?

   a. female parent of a child
   b. opposite of father
   c. one who holds you when you're sick and listens when you really need to talk
   d. All of these are operational definitions.
   e. None of these is an operational definition.

14. Which of these is an analogy?

   a. Each dollar spent for education saves the state money in the long run.
   b. Four thousand dollars was spent on education for each $8,000 that was spent on prisons.
   c. Spending money on prisons instead of education is like spending money to cure diseases that we could prevent.
   d. Dollar for dollar and dime for dime we decrease the decency of our democracy.
   e. Imagine yourself in a prison cell instead of in a college classroom.

15. Visual aids can help the audience because they can show

   a. how things work.
   b. how things look.
   c. how things relate.
   d. all of the above
   e. none of the above

16. Which item gives correct advice about using visual aids?

   a. If you're going to use them, make them complex so they're worth the time and energy of both you and your audience.
   b. Keep them small so you can easily transport them and you won't have to worry about overwhelming yourself with visuals.
   c. Always use complete sentences on visuals; phrases alone aren't enough.
   d. Be sure the visual aid is directly related to your speech; a visual aid that is remotely related should not be used.
   e. Look at your visual aid when you display it and continue looking at it as you speak so your audience will follow your lead and look at it too.

ATCHING II (MOTIVATED SEQUENCE)

elow is a short speech following the steps of the motivated sequence. Match the labels of the motivated equence with the part that fulfills that purpose.

eed **action** **satisfaction** **attention**

isualization

_______________ 1. If someone offered you a place to play in the sand and the sun, a place to relax and warm up, would you take it?

_______________ 2. I know many of you are like me and feeling like it is necessary to get away from it all. You require a place to warm up for a while and a time and a place to give your brain a break from exams.

_______________ 3. Good news! Student services and the credit union have teamed up just for you. During winter break, they are offering a four-day Caribbean adventure at a price even a student can afford.

_______________ 4. Picture yourself on a cruise to the Bahamas, soaking up sun while your classmates shovel snow from their cars. Writing papers and taking exams will be far from your mind.

_______________ 5. Sign up now for the student rates offered by the credit union on this cruise of a lifetime.

TRUE/FALSE

Circle the T or F to indicate whether you believe the statement is true or false. If it is **true**, give a **reason** or an **example**. If it is **false**, **explain** what would make it true.

T F **1.** An outline contains main ideas and shows how they relate to each other and to the thesis.

____

____

T F **2.** Basic speech structure refers to chronological, problem–solution, topical, and cause–effect.

____

____

T F **3.** One purpose of a formal outline is to show the specific purpose of the speech.

____

____

T F **4.** The motivated sequence is a variation of the chronological outline pattern.

____

____

T F **5.** Statistics are a type of transition.

____

____

COMPLETION

Fill in each of the blanks with a word from the list provided. Choose the BEST word for each sentence. There are more words than you will use, but each word will be used only once.

statistics **description** **quotation** **analogy**
hypothetical

1. A/an ______________________ uses word pictures so an audience can visualize an idea.

2. To say that one idea is like another idea is to use a/an ______________________.

3. When it isn't just someone's ideas you want to cite, but the entire memorable way she or he said it, you would choose to use a/an ______________________.

4. To make an idea more specific by making it numerical, it is best to support the idea by ______________________.

5. If an audience is asked to imagine something, rather than be told a true story, the example is ______________________.

TES ON ORGANIZATION AND SUPPORT

CHAPTER 11 ANSWERS TO SELF TEST

MATCHING I (KEY TERMS)

1. j **2.** n **3.** f **4.** k **5.** l
6. i **7.** d **8.** a **9.** o **10.** m
11. g **12.** e **13.** b **14.** h **15.** c

MATCHING II (MOTIVATED SEQUENCE)

16. e **17.** f **18.** c **19.** b **20.** a
21. i **22.** d **23.** j **24.** g **25.** h
26. k **27.** l

MULTIPLE CHOICE

1. d **2.** b **3.** c **4.** a **5.** b
6. e **7.** d **8.** a **9.** d **10.** a
11. e **12.** e **13.** c **14.** c **15.** d
16. d

MATCHING (MOTIVATED SEQUENCE)

1. attention **2.** need **3.** satisfaction **4.** visualization **5.** action

TRUE/FALSE

1. T **2.** F **3.** F **4.** F **5.** F

COMPLETION

1. description **2.** analogy **3.** quotation
4. statistics **5.** hypothetical

ELATED READING

nderstanding Traditional African American Preaching," by Janice D. Hamlet, *Our Voices: Essays in lture, Ethnicity, and Communication: An Intercultural Anthology,* edited by Alberto Gonzalez, rsha Houston, and Victoria Chen (Roxbury Publishing Company, 1994).

EVIEW:

key concept in Chapter 11 is to choose supporting material that will make the points of a speech clear, teresting, memorable, and convincing. Janice D. Hamlet explains the unique features of African nerican preaching and the types of supporting material that enhance this style. Note that an essential aracteristic of and requirement for effective presentations of this type is support in the form of orytelling.

EVIEW:

1. What are the four characteristics of African American preaching style that the author explains?
2. What supporting materials would carry weight with these audiences and not with others?
3. In addition to supporting material, a great deal of this style depends on delivery. What kinds of delivery add credibility to a speaker?
4. Why is interaction (call and response) important for both the speaker and the listeners?
5. What speakers or speeches do you recall that demonstrated the characteristics described in this article?

NOTES ON ORGANIZATION AND SUPPORT

Chapter 12
Presenting Your Message

FTER STUDYING THIS CHAPTER, YOU WILL BETTER UNDERSTAND:

1. The differences among the various types of delivery.
2. The visual and auditory aspects of delivery that help you choose the best type of delivery of a particular speech.
3. The difference between facilitative and debilitative stage fright.
4. The sources of debilitative stage fright.

FTER STUDYING THIS CHAPTER, YOU WILL BE BETTER ABLE TO:

1. Choose the most effective type of delivery for a particular speech.
2. Follow the guidelines for effective extemporaneous, impromptu, manuscript, and memorized speeches.
3. Overcome debilitative stage fright.
4. Offer constructive criticism of others' presentations.

HAPTER 12 SKELETON OUTLINE

his outline can be a helpful study tool to assist you in seeing the order and sequence of the chapter and ie relationship of ideas. Use it to take notes as you read and/or to add concepts presented in lecture.

I. **TYPES OF DELIVERY**
    A. Extemporaneous
        1. Definition
        2. Advantages/uses
        3. Disadvantages
    B. Impromptu
        1. Definition
        2. Advantages/uses
        3. Disadvantages
        4. Points to remember
            a. use time
            b. be original
            c. observe and respond
            d. positive attitude
            e. brevity
    C. Manuscript
        1. Definition
        2. Advantages/uses
        3. Disadvantages
        4. Points to remember
            a. note differences
            b. use short paragraphs
            c. type appropriately

- **d.** paper details
- **e.** rehearse
- **f.** time, speed, ideas

D. Memorized
- **1.** Definition
- **2.** Advantages/uses
- **3.** Disadvantages
- **4.** Important point: practice

II. PRACTICING THE SPEECH

- **A.** Talk
- **B.** Tape
- **C.** Present to mirror
- **D.** Present to people
- **E.** Present in context

III. GUIDELINES FOR DELIVERY

- **A.** Visual aspects
  - **1.** Appearance
  - **2.** Movement
    - **a.** voluntary can replace involuntary
    - **b.** contact with all
  - **3.** Posture
  - **4.** Facial expression
  - **5.** Eye contact
- **B.** Auditory aspects
  - **1.** Volume
  - **2.** Rate
  - **3.** Pitch
  - **4.** Articulation
    - **a.** deletion
    - **b.** substitution
    - **c.** addition
    - **d.** slurring

IV. SPEAKING WITH CONFIDENCE

- **A.** Facilitative and debilitative stage fright
- **B.** Debilitative stage fright sources
  - **1.** previous negative experience
  - **2.** Irrational thinking (fallacies)
    - **a.** catastrophic failure
    - **b.** perfection
    - **c.** approval
    - **d.** overgeneralization
- **C.** Overcoming debilitative stage fright
  - **1.** Be rational
  - **2.** Be receiver-oriented
  - **3.** Be positive
    - **a.** positive statements
    - **b.** visualization
  - **4.** Be prepared

V. OFFERING CONSTRUCTIVE CRITICISM

- **A.** Be complete
- **B.** Be specific
- **C.** Be positive

APTER 12 KEY TERMS

is list of key terms corresponds to those in boldface in your text. Use these lines to write the inition and/or an example of the word on the line next to it.

ition ______________________________

____

iculation ______________________________

____

ilitative stage fright ______________________________

____

etion ______________________________

____

emporaneous speech ______________________________

____

ilitative stage fright ______________________________

____

lacy of approval ______________________________

____

lacy of catastrophic failure ______________________________

____

lacy of overgeneralization ______________________________

____

lacy of perfection ______________________________

____

aging ______________________________

____

npromptu speech ______________________________

____

rational thinking ______________________________

____

manuscript speech ______________________________

____

memorized speech ______________________________

____

pitch ______________________________

____

rate ______________________________

____

slurring ______________________________

____

substitution ______________________________

____

visualization ______________________________

____

NAME ______________________________

HAPTER 12. ACTIVITY 1: DELIVERY STYLES

URPOSE:

o distinguish among delivery styles and determine which style is best suited to various situations.

NSTRUCTIONS:

ead each situation. For each, decide which delivery is best suited to the situation and give your reasons ased on information in the text. Choices: memorized, manuscript, impromptu, extemporaneous.

1. You are asked to give a report in history class. Each student is assigned a topic and must give a five-minute talk to explain and illustrate the concept for the rest of the class.

   Preferred delivery style: ______________________________

   Reasons: ______________________________

   ____

   ____

2. You are a member of a campus transitional mentoring group, helping to mentor high school seniors and encourage them to attend college. You are asked to speak to various student organizations on campus to encourage their members to become mentors to high school students.

   Preferred delivery style: ______________________________

   Reasons: ______________________________

   ____

   ____

3. The local radio station has asked you to present a one-minute public service announcement about an approaching campus concert.

   Preferred delivery style: ______________________________

   Reasons: ______________________________

   ____

   ____

4. You are attending a meeting at work and there is discussion of switching to a new software program. Most people have not used the program, but are favorably impressed and inclined to switch. You used the program in your previous job with disastrous results and you want to share your experience and information to avoid what you think would be a costly mistake. The decision will be made without any further meetings.

   Preferred delivery style: ______________________________

   Reasons: ______________________________

   ____

   ____

5. You are one of six finalists for a job training customer service reps. All six are being called back before the selection committee and asked to make a four-minute presentation about their philosophy of what customer service means in this particular position.

   Preferred delivery style: ______________________________

   Reasons: ____

   ____

   ____

6. Your college is putting together a video collage of all student organizations to be shown to the community to help ease some tensions between the city and the college. Each group has a chance to film a two-minute message. You are asked to be the "speaker" for the two minutes for an organization you belong to.

   Preferred delivery style: ______________________________

   Reasons: ____

   ____

   ____

NAME ______________________________

HAPTER 12. ACTIVITY 2: VOCAL DELIVERY

URPOSE:

o practice auditory aspects of delivery.

NSTRUCTIONS:

o demonstrate various vocal channels, try one of the following two ways.

1. Try to enact each scene below, using ONLY the word "mom." Listen to yourself and record what you think is happening with your auditory aspects of delivery.
2. With a partner, practice saying the word "mom" as if you were saying it in these settings. Listen to your partner and record your observations. Then switch roles. If you are doing it with a partner, do them in random order and see if you can guess each situation, based on vocal characteristics.

1. You come home and are very excited about getting a new job, making the team, or some other big event. You can't wait to tell mom. How would you say "mom" as you burst in the house to tell her?

   What did you notice about

   Volume? ______________________________

   Pitch? ______________________________

   Rate? ______________________________

2. You are really angry with your mom. She has just given you some news that you didn't like (told you she can't pay your tuition anymore, can't loan you her car tonight, can't make it to some event you were counting on her being at). You are frustrated and angry at this change of events. How would you say "mom"?

   What did you notice about

   Volume? ______________________________

   Pitch? ______________________________

   Rate? ______________________________

3. You are scared. You just did something pretty awful that involves your mom and now you need to tell her (you dented her car, broke or ruined something of hers you had borrowed). You are scared and apprehensive, but you need to tell her. You approach her and say "mom."

   What did you notice about

   Volume? ______________________________

   Pitch? ______________________________

   Rate? ______________________________

4. You are a two-year-old (or a twenty-two-year-old) and you are whining about not getting something you want. You want mom to buy something for you and she won't. You whine "mom."

   What did you notice about

   Volume? ______________________________

   Pitch? ______________________________

   Rate? ______________________________

VARIATIONS:

1. Four students line up in the back of the room and each enacts one scenario. Without looking at them, can you identify which one is enacting which scene?
2. Instead of the word "mom," choose nonsense syllables or a word out of context (try "helicopter" or "picture frame") and use these words in the same scenarios to listen for changes in auditory aspects of delivery.

Questions to consider:

1. Compared to others, I consider my volume to be (louder, softer, more varied, less varied) than others. The implications this has for speech delivery are

   ____

   ____

   ____

2. Compared to others, I consider my rate to be (faster, slower, more varied, less varied) than others. The implications this has for speech delivery are

   ____

   ____

   ____

3. Compared to others, I consider my pitch to be (higher, lower, more varied, less varied) than others. The implications this has for speech delivery are

   ____

   ____

   ____

With regard to articulation, I know I have a tendency toward

_______ deletion in words such as ______________________________

_______ substitution in words such as ______________________________

_______ addition in words such as ______________________________

_______ slurring in words such as ______________________________

See text for examples of these common errors. Compare your lists with those of your classmates.

NAME ______________________________

HAPTER 12. ACTIVITY 3: REWRITING IRRATIONAL FALLACIES

URPOSE:

) practice rewriting irrational fallacies.

NSTRUCTIONS:

1. For each item of self-talk below, identify the type of fallacy it represents.
2. Then rewrite what a speaker could say to himself or herself that is more reasonable and rational.

1. I just know I'll blow it. I'll likely start off bad and then never be able to get the delivery going.

   Irrational fallacy: ______________________________

   Rewrite, using more rational thoughts: ______________________________

   ____

   ____

2. My visuals just aren't as good as Melissa's. The coloring isn't quite right and one of my bar graphs is off-center.

   Irrational fallacy: ______________________________

   Rewrite, using more rational thoughts: ______________________________

   ____

   ____

3. I'll probably get a dry mouth and turn red. It'll be obvious to everyone that I'm nervous and scared.

   Irrational fallacy: ______________________________

   Rewrite, using more rational thoughts: ______________________________

   ____

   ____

4. I always blow it when something is real important—like the time I used the wrong name when introducing my boss.

   Irrational fallacy: ______________________________

   Rewrite, using more rational thoughts: ______________________________

   ____

   ____

5. Tim probably won't like the visuals and Jose won't like some of the sources I cite.

Irrational fallacy: ___________________________________

Rewrite, using more rational thoughts: ___________________________________

____

____

NAME ______________________________

CHAPTER 12. ACTIVITY 4: CRITIQUING CLASSMATES

PURPOSE:

To consider the purpose and improve the process of critiquing classmates.

INSTRUCTIONS:

1. Read the paragraph below about critiquing your classmates.
2. Respond to the paragraph by answering the questions at the end.

In Chapter 7, you read about Jack Gibb's understanding of characteristics which promote a defensive or a supportive climate. In critiquing your classmates, you will want to try and be perceived as supportive, which means being perceived as descriptive rather than evaluative, with empathy not neutrality, equality not superiority, spontaneous not manipulative, provisional not certain, and problem-oriented not controlling. Remember, there is less defensiveness when a person believes the evaluation given is appropriate for the context. When students are placed in the role of critiquing their classmates, there may be some discomfort with the role. However, the term *critic* need not have a negative connotation. You can be of help to your classmates, helping them focus on strengths as well as areas that could be improved. Often, describing what you saw and felt is helpful. Try to remember these guidelines:

1. **Accent the praiseworthy and positive.**
   Often speakers are so full of self-criticism for what they wish they'd done, should have done, didn't do, did poorly, that they don't immediately see their strong points.

   Try using:
   I appreciated the way you . . .
   I liked your ability to . . .
   I think . . . is one of your real strengths as a speaker.
   You seemed relaxed as you spoke to us.
   Your introduction made me want to hear more.

2. **Use I-language which is descriptive, not evaluative.**
   Tell what you actually observed, what information you took in through your senses. Sometimes description, not evaluation, is all that is needed. If you do evaluate, be sure to describe first so the person knows what you are referring to.

I-LANGUAGE/DESCRIPTIVE	YOU-LANGUAGE/EVALUATIVE
I couldn't hear you.	You were/weren't loud enough.
I had no trouble hearing you.	
I saw you speak from several different places.	You moved too much.
I felt upset when you used the word "girl" to refer to your secretary.	You were demeaning to women.
I was unclear about your main point.	You didn't make your points clear.
I could see your note cards being tapped and shuffled over and over.	You kept messing with your notes.
I felt offended by your comment on women.	You offended all women.

Try using:

I felt . . .
From my point of view . . .
I couldn't . . . (see, hear, understand, etc.)
It seemed to me . . .
My reaction was . . .

YOUR TURN:

1. What do you especially agree or disagree with from page 331?

2. What are some other guidelines or standards that you think should apply to classmates critiquing each other?

3. What do you especially appreciate from a classmate/critic?

4. What do you especially want a classmate/critic NOT to do?

5. Do you want different things from a classmate in an oral (public, to the class) and in a written (private, to you only) critique? Explain.

Discuss your answers with your classmates and find your areas of agreement.

HAPTER 12. ACTIVITY 5: EXPLORING THE WEB

ISTENING TO AUDITORY ASPECTS OF FAMOUS SPEECHES

o to The History Channel's speech archives at *www.historychannel.com/speeches/index.html.* Choose ur speeches (from over 100 listed) that will give you a mixture of ethnicity, gender, decade, region, and ationality. For each speech, describe the auditory characteristics of the speaker. Notice how the eaker uses volume, rate, pitch, and articulation. From what you hear, how do these characteristics npact the effectiveness of the speaker?

1. Name of speaker: ____________________

Occasion/topic: ____________________

How does the speaker use

Volume? ____________________

Rate? ____________________

Pitch? ____________________

Articulation? ____________________

Note examples of deletion, substitution, addition, slurring, or accents or dialects.

____

____

2. Name of speaker: ____________________

Occasion/topic: ____________________

How does the speaker use

Volume? ____________________

Rate? ____________________

Pitch? ____________________

Articulation? ____________________

Note examples of deletion, substitution, addition, slurring, or accents or dialects.

____

____

3. Name of speaker: ______________________

Occasion/topic: ______________________

How does the speaker use

Volume? ______________________

Rate? ______________________

Pitch? ______________________

Articulation? ______________________

Note examples of deletion, substitution, addition, slurring, or accents or dialects.

____

____

4. Name of speaker: ______________________

Occasion/topic: ______________________

How does the speaker use

Volume? ______________________

Rate? ______________________

Pitch? ______________________

Articulation? ______________________

Note examples of deletion, substitution, addition, slurring, or accents or dialects.

____

____

NAME ______________________________

HAPTER 12 SELF TEST

ATCHING I (KEY TERMS)

atch each term listed on the left with its correct definition from the column on the right.

_____ **1.** addition
_____ **2.** articulation
_____ **3.** debilitative stage fright
_____ **4.** deletion
_____ **5.** extemporaneous speech
_____ **6.** facilitative stage fright
_____ **7.** fallacy of approval
_____ **8.** fallacy of catastrophic failure
_____ **9.** fallacy of overgeneralization
_____ **10.** fallacy of perfection
_____ **11.** visualization
_____ **12.** impromptu speech
_____ **13.** irrational thinking
_____ **14.** manuscript speech
_____ **15.** memorized speech
_____ **16.** pitch
_____ **17.** rate
_____ **18.** slurring
_____ **19.** substitution

a. the irrational belief that the worst possible outcome will probably occur
b. the irrational belief that a worthwhile communicator should be able to handle every situation with complete confidence and skill
c. the speed at which a speaker utters words
d. the irrational belief that it is vital to win the sanction or endorsement of virtually every person a communicator deals with
e. a speech that is read word-for-word from a prepared text
f. an articulation error of leaving out sounds of words
g. a speech that is planned in advance but presented in a direct, conversational manner
h. a technique for self-improvement that involves one's picturing in his/her mind the successful completion of a task
i. broad category of beliefs that have no basis in reality or logic; one source of debilitative stage fright
j. the articulation error that involves overlapping the end of one word with the beginning of the next
k. irrational beliefs in (usually negative) conclusions based on limited evidence or communicators exaggerating their shortcomings
l. intense level of anxiety about speaking before an audience, resulting in poor performance
m. a moderate level of anxiety about speaking before an audience that helps improve performance
n. an articulation error of putting in extra parts to words
o. a speech given "off the top of one's head" without advance preparation
p. the process of pronouncing words distinctly and carefully
q. a speech learned and delivered by rote without a written text or note cards
r. the highness or lowness of one's voice
s. the articulation error that involves replacing part of a word with an incorrect sound

MULTIPLE CHOICE

Choose the BEST response from those listed.

1. A certain candidate remarked that his only three mistakes in his first political speech were that h read it, read it poorly, and it wasn't worth reading. Chances are he used which type of delivery?

a. impromptu
b. manuscript
c. memorized
d. extemporaneous
e. none of the above

2. Which of these describes extemporaneous delivery?

a. It is off the cuff with no preparation.
b. It is carefully prepared and rehearsed word for word.
c. It is carefully prepared, then presented conversationally.
d. It is read from a teleprompter.
e. It is spontaneous and uses no notes.

3. Which delivery style is generally accepted as the most appropriate and effective for the college classroom?

a. impromptu
b. manuscript
c. memorized
d. extemporaneous
e. All work equally well in the average college classroom.

4. If you need to be grammatically precise, keep an exact time limit, or have your speech be part of legal record, the best delivery style would be _________.

a. impromptu
b. manuscript
c. memorized
d. extemporaneous
e. All would work equally well.

5. If you need to give a memorized speech, the single most important piece of advice is:

a. Practice.
b. Type the manuscript to practice from.
c. Use elaborate rather than succinct language.
d. Make the delivery more formal than the speech.
e. All of the above are significant pieces of advice.

6. In using a manuscript delivery, all of the following guidelines are presented in your text EXCEPT:

a. Use longer paragraphs so you don't seem choppy and disjointed.
b. Rehearse until you can read whole lines without looking at the manuscript.
c. Vary your speed.
d. Type the manuscript and underline words you want to emphasize.
e. Use stiff paper that won't blow away or crumple easily.

7. You have been asked to give a quick reaction to a speaker at a small committee meeting. Which style would you use?

a. impromptu
b. manuscript
c. memorized
d. extemporaneous
e. All would work equally well.

8. Movement as a part of delivery enables you to

a. replace involuntary actions with voluntary ones.
b. involve more members of the audience in the action zone.
c. add emphasis to your message.
d. all of the above
e. none of the above

9. According to Marcy Huber, what should you do when presenting to cross-cultural audiences?

a. Use more silence and pauses.
b. Use plenty of idioms.
c. Humor is universal; use a lot of it.
d. Be prepared for numerous questions; most cultures are very comfortable with them.
e. all of the above

10. Maintaining eye contact with your audience usually

a. convinces audience members that you are interested in them.
b. overwhelms or intimidates audience members.
c. helps you do a "reality check" regarding how the audience perceives you.
d. both b and c
e. both a and c

11. As you speed up or become louder, your pitch tends to

a. vary greatly.
b. rise.
c. fall.
d. rise when you speed up, fall when you become louder.
e. fall when you speed up, rise when you become louder.

12. The most important thing for a speaker to remember when considering volume, rate, and pitch is to

a. use variety and use them for emphasis.
b. keep them low, slow, and low, respectively.
c. keep them all as high as possible.
d. concentrate on volume; rate and pitch will fall in place.
e. None of the above represents sound advice.

13. Addition, substitution, slurring, and deletion are all types of problems with

a. volume.
b. emphasis.
c. articulation.
d. visual aspects of delivery.
e. movement.

14. With regard to facilitative stage fright,

a. it doesn't exist.
b. it is far more common than debilitative stage fright.
c. it can be used to aid your speech delivery.
d. it can help you perform at your top capacity.
e. both c and d.

✓ **15.** Debilitative stage fright is frequently caused by

a. irrational thinking.
b. previous negative experience.
c. rationality and receiver-orientation.
d. both a and b.
e. both b and c.

MATCHING II (FALLACIES)

Match the types of fallacies with the label for that type of debilitative and irrational thinking that it represents. One will be used more than once.

catastrophic failure **approval** **perfection** **overgeneralization**

________ **1.** I sure messed up my visual aids; that one slide was upside down. [Four different visuals were used.]

________ **2.** If I can't get an A on this speech, I'm just a complete failure.

________ **3.** The instructor probably won't like my topic and I'll probably get a D for the course. If I get a D for the course, I'll never graduate. If I never graduate . . .

________ **4.** [After **one** of five jokes wasn't laughed at] The audience never laughs at my jokes.

________ **5.** Everyone just has to like my speech. I can't stand the thought of even one person in the class thinking I did a poor job.

TRUE/FALSE

Circle the T or F to indicate whether you believe the statement is true or false. If it is **true**, give a **reason** or an **example**. If it is **false**, **explain** what would make it true.

T F **1.** When asked to respond to a classmate's speech, begin by giving suggestions for improvement and follow with very general remarks.

____

____

T F **2.** Saying "goin'" or "runnin'" instead of "going" and "running" are examples of substitution.

____

____

T F **3.** Receiver-orientation refers to concentrating on the audience rather than on yourself.

____

____

T F **4.** If you expect your speech to be perfect and keep telling yourself it has to be, you are likely to experience facilitative stage fright.

____

____

T F **5.** Practice your speech by actually talking through the whole thing, not just saying, "I'll give some examples here," but speaking through the examples.

____

____

COMPLETION

Fill in each of the blanks with a word from the list provided. Choose the BEST word for each sentence. There are more words than you will use, but each word will be used only once.

auditory	**impromptu**	**fallacy**	**yourself**
visual	**rational**	**memorized**	**the audience**

1. A/an ____________________ is a type of irrational thinking.

2. Being asked to give an immediate response to another student's speech is an example of a type of ____________________ speech you will likely make in this class.

3. The best way to avoid debilitative stage fright from fallacies is to replace those thoughts with ____________________ thinking.

4. Being receiver-oriented is a way to take the focus off of ____________________.

5. Posture, movement, and eye contact are all part of the ____________________ aspects of delivery.

CHAPTER 12 ANSWERS TO SELF TEST

MATCHING I (KEY TERMS)

1. n	**2.** p	**3.** l	**4.** f	**5.** g
6. m	**7.** d	**8.** a	**9.** k	**10.** b
11. h	**12.** o	**13.** i	**14.** e	**15.** q
16. r	**17.** c	**18.** j	**19.** s	

MULTIPLE CHOICE

1. b	**2.** c	**3.** d	**4.** b	**5.** a
6. a	**7.** a	**8.** d	**9.** a	**10.** e
11. b	**12.** a	**13.** c	**14.** e	**15.** d

MATCHING II (FALLACIES)

1. overgeneralization	**2.** perfection	**3.** catastrophic failure
4. overgeneralization	**5.** approval	

TRUE/FALSE

1. F	**2.** F	**3.** T	**4.** F	**5.** T

COMPLETION

1. fallacy	**2.** impromptu	**3.** rational	**4.** yourself	**5.** visual

ELATED READING

Beating the Paranoia of Presentations," by Lynn O'Rourke Hayes, *Lodging Hospitality* 47, no. 9)ctober 1991): 38, 40.

REVIEW:

tage fright. Communication apprehension. CA. Presentation Paranoia. It goes by a number of names ıd most of us can recall at least one attack of it. However, as Chapter 12 points out, stage fright can be ebilitative or facilitative. The author of this article describes her journey from debilitative to facilitative age fright, providing anecdotes that we can identify with and advice that we can heed.

EVIEW:

1. What experiences have you had that parallel or top the author's experiences as described in the opening paragraphs of this article?
2. According to the author, what part does awareness of your emotions and permission to experience them play in dealing with stage fright?
3. List all of the physical symptoms of stage fright given in the article and add to them.
4. How do the barriers listed in this article compare to the irrational fallacies discussed in Chapter 12 of our text?
5. Summarize the author's advice and compare and contrast it with that in the text.

NOTES ON PRESENTING YOUR MESSAGE

Chapter 13
Informative Speaking

FTER STUDYING THIS CHAPTER, YOU WILL BETTER UNDERSTAND:

1. The difference between an informative and a persuasive speech topic.
2. The need for having a specific informative purpose.
3. The significance of creating information hunger.
4. The importance of using clear language, developing organizational strategies, and emphasizing key points.
5. The significance of generating audience involvement.

FTER STUDYING THIS CHAPTER, YOU WILL BE BETTER ABLE TO:

1. Categorize informative speeches by format, content, and purpose.
2. Formulate an effective informative purpose statement and create "information hunger."
3. Use the strategies outlined in this chapter to organize information in a clear and understandable manner, emphasize important points, and use clear language.
4. Develop effective supporting material.
5. Generate audience involvement.

HAPTER 13 SKELETON OUTLINE

his outline can be a helpful study tool to assist you in seeing the order and sequence of the chapter and ie relationship of ideas. Use it to take notes as you read and/or to add concepts presented in lecture.

I. CATEGORIZING TYPES OF INFORMATIVE SPEAKING

- **A.** Format
  - **1.** Briefings
  - **2.** Reports
- **B.** Content
  - **1.** Objects
  - **2.** Processes
  - **3.** Events
  - **4.** Concepts
- **C.** Purpose
  - **1.** Descriptions
  - **2.** Explanations
  - **3.** Instructions

II. INFORMATIVE VS. PERSUASIVE TOPICS

- **A.** Informative topics tend to be noncontroversial.
- **B.** Informative speaking is not intended to change audience attitudes.

III. TECHNIQUES OF INFORMATIVE SPEAKING

- **A.** Define a specific informative purpose.
  - **1.** Informative purpose statement.
  - **2.** Clear thesis

B. Create information hunger by emphasizing physical, identity, social, and practical needs.
C. Make it easy to listen.
   1. Limit information
   2. Use familiar to lead to unfamiliar
   3. Use simple to lead to complex
D. Emphasize important points.
   1. Repetition
   2. Signposts
E. Use a clear organization.
   1. Introduction
   2. Body (organize, use internal summary and review and transitions)
   3. Conclusion
F. Use support effectively.
G. Use clear language.
   1. Precise, simple vocabulary
   2. Avoid jargon
H. Generate audience involvement.
   1. Audience participation
   2. Volunteers
   3. Question-and-answer period
      a. focus on substance
      b. paraphrase
      c. avoid defensiveness
      d. answer briefly

CHAPTER 13 KEY TERMS

This list of key terms corresponds to those in boldface in your text. Use these lines to write the definition and/or an example of the word on the line next to it.

audience involvement ______________________________

____

audience participation ______________________________

____

briefing ______________________________

____

general needs ______________________________

____

information hunger ______________________________

____

informative purpose statement ______________________________

____

ɔort ______________________________

____

ɡnpost ______________________________

____

ecific needs ______________________________

____

NOTES ON INFORMATIVE SPEAKING

NAME ______________________

[CH]APTER 13. ACTIVITY 1: CREATING INFORMATION HUNGER

[PU]RPOSE:

[To] illustrate ways to create information hunger.

[IN]STRUCTIONS:

[Fo]r each speech being prepared, list ways you could create information hunger by appealing to the [ph]ysical, identity, social, or practical needs of that audience.

[Ex]ample:

[Yo]u are speaking to a high-risk group about the rising incidence of Hepatitis B. What needs would you [ap]peal to? How?

____

____

____

1. You are speaking to a group of high school students about the rising incidence of teen pregnancy. What needs would you appeal to? How?

   ____

   ____

   ____

2. You are speaking to a group of students about the new registration procedures being implemented. What needs would you appeal to? How?

   ____

   ____

   ____

3. You are speaking to co-workers about the changes in health care providers. What needs would you appeal to? How?

   ____

   ____

   ____

4. You are speaking to a group of expectant parents about how the choice of names for a child affects him/her for life. What needs would you appeal to? How?

   ____

   ____

   ____

5. You are speaking to a low-risk group about the rising incidence of AIDS. What needs would you appeal to? How?

6. You are speaking to an incoming group of freshmen about the legal aspects of acquaintance rape. What needs would you appeal to? How?

7. You are speaking to high school students on scholarship opportunities. What needs would you appeal to? How?

8. You are speaking to foreign students about the medical care/medical insurance situation in the United States. What needs would you appeal to? How?

9. You are speaking to members of a community group about your travel to a recent convention they financed for you. What needs would you appeal to? How?

10. You are speaking to employees about the need to be aware of what behaviors constitute sexual harassment. What needs would you appeal to? How?

NAME ______________________________

HAPTER 13. ACTIVITY 2: CRITIQUE SHEET

URPOSE:

) critique an informative speech.

NSTRUCTIONS:

eview the information on critiquing a classmate from Activity 4 in Chapter 12. Then, as directed by our instructor, fill in this sheet while listening to a classmate's speech or public videotaped speech. Try) use specific details.

peaker's name ______________________ Topic ______________________

1. In my opinion, the strengths of the introduction were ______________________

____

____

2. In my opinion, the introduction would be better if ______________________

____

____

3. It seemed to me that the speech was/was not clearly organized because ______________________

____

____

4. What I liked about the visual aids and supporting material was ______________________

____

____

5. What I think would improve the visual aids and supporting material is ______________________

____

____

6. I think the strong points of the delivery were ______________________

____

____

7. I think the delivery would be improved by ______________________

____

____

8. I think the best thing about the conclusion was ______________________

____

____

9. I think the conclusion would be improved by ______________________

____

____

10. Overall, what I liked best about the presentation was ______________________

____

____

NAME ______________________________

HAPTER 13. ACTIVITY 3: ANALYZING A SPEECH

JRPOSE:

› analyze a speaker from outside class.

ISTRUCTIONS:

rrange to listen to an outside speaker on campus or in the community. Fill in the following.

›eaker's name: ______________________________

›cation of speech: ______________________________

ccasion: ______________________________

›pic or title: ______________________________

escribe the intended audience: (Was this for a particular group or club? open to the public? for profit?)

____

1. Was there a clear introduction? What technique was used? Did it get attention and preview the speech?

____

____

____

2. Was the speech clearly organized? Could you follow the main points? Could you always tell the main idea? What type of outline was used?

____

____

____

3. What types of support were used? Did the speaker use varied and appropriate forms of support?

____

____

____

4. Were there previews, transitions, and internal summaries? What kind? How effective were they?

____

____

____

5. Did the delivery enhance the speech or detract from it? What was especially good about the delivery? What would improve it?

6. Was there a clear conclusion? What technique was used? Did it get reviewed and clearly bring the speech to a close?

7. Other overall impressions or comments:

NAME ____________________

HAPTER 13. ACTIVITY 4: PRACTICING DELIVERY

URPOSE:

ɔ review a video of one's own speech to become aware of strengths and weaknesses in delivery.

ISTRUCTIONS:

1. Videotape yourself giving a speech.
2. Watch the whole video with sound, then watch a part of the video without sound and fill out the following.

1. My first reactions to seeing myself on this video were ____________________

____

____

____

2. While watching myself without the sound, I noticed this about my

eye contact ____________________

____

____

hands/gestures ____________________

____

____

movement ____________________

____

____

facial expression ____________________

____

____

3. The four things that I think I did well are:

a. ____________________

____

b. ____________________

____

c. ______________________________

____

d. ______________________________

____

4. I think my presentation would be improved for this audience if I would:

____

____

____

____

____

____

____

NAME ______________________

CHAPTER 13. ACTIVITY 5: EXPLORING THE WEB

ANALYZING AN INFORMATIVE SPEECH

Choose a speech from any of the Web sites listed in Chapter 13. Gifts of Speech is a particularly good site to explore: *http://gos.sbc.edu/*. Here you can choose a speech of interest to you from over 200 speeches by a variety of influential women. The following speech found there is recommended for this exercise: Address to the People of Prague, "Obecni Dum—A Moment of Celebration and of Dedication," by Madeleine Albright, July 14, 1997.

What is the informative purpose? ______________________

____

What is the thesis? ______________________

____

In this speech, what technique is used in the introduction? ______________________

____

How does the speaker create information hunger? ______________________

____

What needs (physical, identity, social, and practical needs) are used to create information hunger?

____

____

Give an example of how the speaker limits information. ______________________

____

Give an example of how the speaker uses something familiar to lead to something unfamiliar.

____

____

Give an example of the speaker using something simple to lead to something more complex.

____

____

How does the speaker emphasize important points?

Can you find an example of the speaker using repetition? ______________________

____

Can you find an example of the speaker using signposts? ______________________

____

Give examples of internal summaries, reviews, and transitions:

internal summaries ____

____

reviews ____

____

What transitions are used? Are they effective? Why or why not? ______________

____

____

HAPTER 13 SELF TEST

ATCHING (KEY TERMS)

atch each term listed on the left with its correct definition from the column on the right.

_____ **1.** audience involvement
_____ **2.** audience participation
_____ **3.** briefing
_____ **4.** general needs
_____ **5.** information hunger
_____ **6.** informative purpose statement
_____ **7.** report
_____ **8.** signpost
_____ **9.** specific needs

a. audience desire to learn information created by the speaker
b. phrase that emphasizes the importance of upcoming material in a speech
c. needs of a particular audience as opposed to general needs
d. purpose statement limited to stress audience knowledge or ability or both, not action or change of behavior
e. broad category of methods to encourage audience members to actively participate in some part of the speech process
f. informative speech which presents information from an investigation in an expanded way
g. needs all humans share
h. type of informative speech in which large amounts of information are condensed for a particular audience
i. a technique of audience involvement in which audience members actually do something during the speech

ULTIPLE CHOICE

hoose the BEST response from those listed.

1. Which is true of an informative speech?

a. It tends to change the audience's attitudes.
b. It tries to move the audience to action.
c. It tries to sway the audience's opinions.
d. It tends to be noncontroversial.
e. It is very persuasive.

2. Speeches which explain "how to" do something, are called ________.

a. instructions
b. descriptions
c. explanations
d. events
e. objects

3. You can create information hunger by

a. responding to general needs of the audience.
b. responding to specific needs of the audience.
c. responding to self-actualization needs of the audience.
d. all of the above
e. none of the above

4. A speech on how to have more friends and meet people more readily appeals most to

   a. physical needs.
   b. safety needs.
   c. social needs.
   d. esteem needs.
   e. self-actualization needs.

5. In order to make it easy for the audience to listen, a speaker should

   a. present as much information as possible to keep the audience interested.
   b. present only unfamiliar information; audiences will be bored with the familiar.
   c. use simple information to build up understanding of complex information.
   d. all of the above
   e. none of the above

6. One way to **create emphasis** in your speech is to stress important points through

   a. repetition.
   b. use of signposts.
   c. a clear introduction.
   d. paraphrasing confusing questions.
   e. both a and b

7. Detailed descriptions, examples, statistics, and definitions are important types of

   a. introductory materials.
   b. supporting materials.
   c. transition materials.
   d. concluding materials.
   e. none of the above

8. With regard to the use of language, the following advice was given in the text:

   a. Use a complex vocabulary to show your competence.
   b. Try to choose words that are obscure.
   c. Use precise and simple words to convey thoughts.
   d. Use jargon to demonstrate your expertise, especially to outsiders.
   e. Use unusual, little-known words to spice up your speech.

9. Which of these is a way to encourage audience involvement in your speech?

   a. audience participation
   b. use of volunteers from the audience
   c. question-and-answer sessions
   d. all of the above
   e. None of the above encourages true audience involvement.

10. Which of these **does not** demonstrate audience involvement?

   a. In a speech about skin tone, ask audience members to pinch their elbow skin and explain how to judge skin tone from the number of seconds it takes for the skin to "pop" back.
   b. In a speech about blindness, ask audience members to close their eyes for twenty seconds.
   c. In a speech about self-concept, ask members of the audience to write down their five "best" traits.
   d. All of these represent examples of audience involvement.
   e. None of these is an appropriate use of audience involvement.

1. When conducting a question-and-answer session, the following guidelines are appropriate EXCEPT:

a. Listen for the substance or big idea of the question.
b. Paraphrase confusing questions before answering.
c. If the questioner is attacking you personally, use a subtle attack rather than give a defensive answer.
d. Answer as briefly as possible.
e. Avoid defensive reactions by responding to the substance.

2. Speeches to inform are often classified in which way?

a. format
b. content
c. purpose
d. all of the above
e. none of the above

3. "We've been talking about ways to enhance our effectiveness at work. **Now here's the real important thing to remember . . .**" Those words represent

a. a signpost.
b. audience involvement.
c. format.
d. repetition.
e. supporting material.

4. During a question-and-answer session, you are asked, "So what about those layoff rumors?" A paraphrase would be

a. There is no truth to those rumors.
b. I'll need to let my supervisor address that concern.
c. Are you asking me to comment on whether or not I know if there is truth to the rumors?
d. The rumors surface every time we bring out a new product line because people fear the loss of their jobs. What's your concern?
e. All of these represent different types of paraphrases.

5. A speech about racism in the United States would be classified by content as a speech about __________.

a. an object
b. a process
c. an event
d. a concept
e. an instruction

RUE/FALSE

ircle the T or F to indicate whether you believe the statement is true or false. If it is **true,** give a **reason** an **example**. If it is **false, explain** what would make it true.

F **1.** One job of the audience is to create information hunger.

____

____

T F 2. An important characteristic of a speech is that it should use more formal, complex langua than either writing or conversation.

____

____

T F 3. A good, specific, informative purpose will state what results the speaker wants.

____

____

T F 4. There is only one way to generate audience involvement in a speech.

____

____

T F 5. Repetition is inappropriate in a speech because it leads to redundancy and bores the audience.

____

____

COMPLETION

Fill in each of the blanks with a word from the list provided. Choose the BEST word for each sentence. There are more words than you will use, but each word will be used only once.

needs	**briefings**	**purposes**	**signposts**
volunteers	**contents**	**descriptions**	

1. __________________ condense information, reports expand it.

2. Asking for __________________ is a way to generate audience involvement.

3. A speaker can create information hunger by appealing to listeners' __________________.

4. One way a speaker can emphasize important points for the audience is to use

   __________________.

5. Descriptions, explanations, and instructions are all ways to classify informative speeches accordin

   to __________________.

NOTES ON INFORMATIVE SPEAKING

CHAPTER 13 ANSWERS TO SELF TEST

MATCHING (KEY TERMS)

1. e **2.** i **3.** h **4.** g **5.** a
6. d **7.** f **8.** b **9.** c

MULTIPLE CHOICE

1. d **2.** a **3.** d **4.** c **5.** c
6. e **7.** b **8.** c **9.** d **10.** d
11. c **12.** d **13.** a **14.** c **15.** d

TRUE/FALSE

1. F **2.** F **3.** T **4.** F **5.** F

COMPLETION

1. briefings **2.** volunteers **3.** needs **4.** signposts **5.** purposes

ELATED READING

emarks by President Clinton at the state funeral of the Prime Minister of Israel, Yitzhak Rabin at Har erzl Cemetery, Jerusalem, Israel, on November 6, 1995 may be found at *tp://www.pub.whitehouse.gov/uri-res/I2R?urn:pdi://oma.eop.gov.us/1995/11/6/2.text.17.*

REVIEW:

November 1995, the world was shocked to hear of the assassination of Prime Minister Yitzhak Rabin ıly minutes after he had appeared at a peace rally. Less than two weeks before that he had attended an istoric peace-signing ceremony. In the grief-filled days that followed, there was much talk about hether hate speech and hate-filled words had been used to bring about his martyrdom. As world aders and family members gathered for his funeral, President Clinton used words to help heal wounds ıd comfort the grieving.

eulogy is a special type of speech, and as you read this one, you will see that it does several things the xt suggests all good speeches do: it is easy to listen to, emphasizes important points, uses a clear ructure, employs support material effectively, and utilizes clear language.

EVIEW:

1. What special goals and purposes did this speech accomplish?
2. Identify all types of supporting materials. What is the impact of these choices? Why are the neck tie anecdotes so effective?
3. What support is used to make the contrast between the power of words and the power of deeds? How is it emphasized that Rabin understood both?
4. How is repetition used for key points?
5. Point out evidence that the particular audience, occasion, and speaker are all taken into account in this address.

NOTES ON INFORMATIVE SPEAKING

Chapter 14
Persuasive Speaking

AFTER STUDYING THIS CHAPTER, YOU WILL BETTER UNDERSTAND:

1. That persuasion involves important ethical questions.
2. The difference between propositions of fact, value, and policy.
3. The difference between the goals of convincing and actuating.
4. The difference between direct and indirect approaches.
5. The basic concepts of persuasive strategy.
6. The importance of setting a clear persuasive purpose.
7. The importance of adapting to your audience.
8. The components of personal credibility.
9. The types of fallacies common in persuasion.

AFTER STUDYING THIS CHAPTER, YOU WILL BE BETTER ABLE TO:

1. Formulate an effective persuasive strategy to convince or actuate an audience.
2. Formulate your persuasive strategy based on ethical guidelines.
3. Bolster your credibility as a speaker by enhancing your competence, character, and charisma.
4. Build persuasive arguments with common ground, solid evidence, and careful reasoning.
5. Organize a persuasive speech for greatest audience effect.
6. Recognize and avoid the use of fallacies.

CHAPTER 14 SKELETON OUTLINE

This outline can be a helpful study tool to assist you in seeing the order and sequence of the chapter and the relationship of ideas. Use it to take notes as you read and/or to add concepts presented in lecture.

I. **CHARACTERISTICS OF PERSUASION**
   A. Persuasion is not coercive.
   B. Persuasion is usually incremental (explained by social judgment theory).
      1. Anchor
      2. Latitudes of acceptance
      3. Latitudes of rejection
      4. Latitudes of noncommitment
   C. Persuasion is interactive.
   D. Persuasion can be ethical.
      1. Definition: ethical persuasion
      2. Unethical persuasion (Table14-1)
      3. Disadvantage of unethical communication

II. **CATEGORIZING TYPES OF PERSUASION**
   A. By proposition
      1. Fact

- 2. Value
- 3. Policy
- B. By desired outcome
  - 1. Convincing
    - a. reinforce
    - b. begin to shift/consider the possibility
  - 2. Actuating
    - a. adoption
    - b. discontinuance
- C. By directness of approach
  - 1. Direct persuasion
  - 2. Indirect persuasion

III. CREATING THE PERSUASIVE MESSAGE

- A. Set clear, persuasive purpose
- B. Structure the message
  - 1. Describe the problem
    - a. nature
    - b. effect on audience
  - 2. Describe the solution
    - a. workability
    - b. advantages
  - 3. Describe desired audience response
    - a. what can audience do?
    - b. what are rewards?
  - 4. Adapting the model persuasive structure
- C. Use solid evidence
  - 1. Support claim
  - 2. Cite sources
    - a. credentials
    - b. currency
- D. Avoid fallacies
  - 1. Attack on the person (ad hominem)
  - 2. Reduction to the absurd (reductio ad absurdum) and straw man argument
  - 3. Either/or
  - 4. False cause (post hoc ergo propter hoc)
  - 5. Appeal to authority (argumentum ad verecundiam)
  - 6. Bandwagon appeal (argumentum ad populum)

IV. ADAPTING TO THE AUDIENCE (TARGET AUDIENCE)

- A. Establish common ground
- B. Organize for expected response
- C. Adapt to hostile audience
  - 1. Show understanding
  - 2. Use appropriate humor

V. BUILD CREDIBILITY

- A. Credibility is based on perception, not objective
  - 1. Initial
  - 2. Derived
  - 3. Terminal
- B. Three c's
  - 1. Competence
  - 2. Character
  - 3. Charisma

HAPTER 14 KEY TERMS

nis list of key terms corresponds to those in boldface in your text. Use these lines to write the efinition and/or an example of the word on the line next to it.

tuating __________

hominum fallacy __________

nchor __________

ppeal to authority __________

rgumentum ad populum __________

rgumentum ad verecundiam __________

andwagon appeal __________

haracter __________

harisma __________

ommon ground __________

ompetence __________

onvincing __________

credibility __________

direct persuasion ______________________________

____

either/or fallacy ______________________________

____

emotional evidence ______________________________

____

ethical persuasion ______________________________

____

evidence ______________________________

____

fallacy ______________________________

____

false cause fallacy ______________________________

____

indirect persuasion ______________________________

____

latitude of acceptance ______________________________

____

latitude of noncommitment ______________________________

____

latitude of rejection ______________________________

____

motivated sequence ______________________________

____

persuasion ______________________________

____

post hoc ergo propter hoc ______________________________

____

oposition of fact ______________________________

____

oposition of policy ______________________________

____

oposition of value ______________________________

____

ductio ad absurdum ______________________________

____

duction to the absurd ______________________________

____

cial judgment theory ______________________________

____

rategy to actuate ______________________________

____

rategy to convince ______________________________

____

raw man fallacy ______________________________

____

rget audience ______________________________

____

NOTES ON PERSUASIVE SPEAKING

NAME ______________________________

HAPTER 14. ACTIVITY 1: LATITUDES

URPOSE:

ɔ differentiate between latitudes of acceptance, noncommitment, and rejection.

ISTRUCTIONS:

ssume that each of the statements below represents an anchor position for your audience. For each of ıe anchors below, write statements which would likely fall within the audience's latitudes of cceptance, noncommitment, and rejection.

xample:

nchor: Capital punishment is wrong because it may be mistaken identity.

iews within their latitude of acceptance:

The state taking a life is wrong.

Taking life is wrong.

iews within their latitude of noncommitment:

If someone confesses freely and wants the death penalty, it might be okay.

iews within their latitude of rejection:

An eye for an eye, a tooth for a tooth.

If someone commits murder, it is okay for the state to take his/her life.

1. **Anchor:** Minorities are treated unfairly in juvenile justice systems.

   Views within their latitude of acceptance:

   ____

   ____

   Views within their latitude of noncommitment:

   ____

   ____

   Views within their latitude of rejection:

   ____

   ____

2. **Anchor:** National health care is fair for the majority of people.

   Views within their latitude of acceptance:

   ____

   ____

Views within their latitude of noncommitment:

____

____

Views within their latitude of rejection:

____

____

3. **Anchor:** Alcoholism is a disease which can be treated.

Views within their latitude of acceptance:

____

____

Views within their latitude of noncommitment:

____

____

Views within their latitude of rejection:

____

____

4. **Anchor:** U.S. involvement in Kosovo harms the United States and Europe.

Views within their latitude of acceptance:

____

____

Views within their latitude of noncommitment:

____

____

Views within their latitude of rejection:

____

____

NAME ______________________

[CH]APTER 14. ACTIVITY 2: FACT, VALUE, OR POLICY

[PU]RPOSES:

1. To construct propositions of fact, value, and policy.
2. To demonstrate that any topic may lead to one of three types of propositions.

[IN]STRUCTIONS:

1. Choose four of these topics or create your own.
2. For each topic, create a proposition of fact, of value, and of policy ON THE SAME TOPIC.

[Fu]nding presidential campaigns
[Do]wnsizing by corporate America
[Us]e of animals for research
[Ve]getarian lifestyle
[Ba]nning fraternities and sororities on campus
[Po]pulation explosion
Euro: Currency for Western Europe
Justice for juveniles
Saving the environment
Funding for Olympic athletes
Delinquent dads/child support
Part-time students

[Ex]ample:

[To]pic: E-mail

[Pr]oposition of fact: E-mail is not private.

[Pr]oposition of value: It is better to use e-mail than any other channel in business.

[Pr]oposition of policy: The United States should institute national laws regulating privacy in use of e-mail.

1. Topic: ______________________

   Proposition of fact: ______________________

   Proposition of value: ______________________

   Proposition of policy: ______________________

2. Topic: ______________________

   Proposition of fact: ______________________

   Proposition of value: ______________________

   Proposition of policy: ______________________

3. Topic: ______________________

   Proposition of fact: ______________________

   Proposition of value: ______________________

   Proposition of policy: ______________________

4. Topic: ____________________

Proposition of fact: ____________________

Proposition of value: ____________________

Proposition of policy: ____________________

NAME ______________________________

IAPTER 14. ACTIVITY 3: CRITIQUE SHEET

RPOSE:

critique a speech of a classmate or public figure (video).

ISTRUCTIONS:

hile listening to the speech, fill in the critique sheet.

eaker's name ______________________ **Topic** ______________________

1. In my opinion, the strengths of the introduction were ______________________

____

____

2. The speaker did/did not establish common ground with the audience by ______________________

____

____

3. It seemed to me that the speech was/was not clearly organized because ______________________

____

____

4. What I liked about the visual aids and supporting material was ______________________

____

____

5. What I think would improve the visual aids and supporting material is ______________________

____

____

6. An effective persuasive strategy and logical and emotional appeals were/were not evident by

____

____

____

7. The speaker did/did not establish credibility by ______________________

____

____

8. I think the strong points of the delivery were ______________________________

____

____

9. I think delivery would be improved by ______________________________

____

____

10. I think the best thing about the conclusion was ______________________________

____

____

11. Strengths and weaknesses of the conclusion: ______________________________

____

____

12. Overall, what I liked best about the presentation was ______________________________

____

____

NAME ______________________________

HAPTER 14. ACTIVITY 4: SELF-CRITIQUE

RPOSE:

- review a video of your own speech to become aware of strengths and weaknesses.

STRUCTIONS:

1. Videotape yourself as you give a speech.
2. Watch the whole video with sound, then watch a part of the video without sound and fill out the following.

1. My first reactions to seeing myself on this video were ______________________________

____

____

____

2. While watching myself without the sound, I noticed this about my

eye contact ______________________________

____

____

hands/gestures ______________________________

____

____

movement ______________________________

____

____

facial expression ______________________________

____

____

3. The four things that I think I did well are:

a. ______________________________

____

b. ______________________________

____

c. ______________________________

____

d. ______________________________

____

4. I think my presentation would be improved for this audience if I would:

____

____

____

____

____

____

____

NAME ____________________

HAPTER 14. ACTIVITY 5: EXPLORING THE WEB

NALYZING SPEECHES BY TYPES OF PROPOSITIONS, FALLACIES, AUDIENCE ADAPTATION

1. Choose a topic of interest to you from The Douglass Archive at *http://douglass.speech.nwu.edu/*. Read the speech and record the following:

   Speech title: ____________________

   Speaker: ____________________ Date: ____________________

   Topic: ____________________

   Type of proposition (fact, value, policy): ____________________

   Main proposition of speech (in the words of the speech or paraphrased):

   ____

   ____

   ____

   Can you find examples of any of these fallacies? Attack on the person (ad hominem), reduction to the absurd (reductio ad absurdum) and straw man argument, either/or, false cause (post hoc ergo propter hoc), appeal to authority (argumentum ad verecundiam), bandwagon appeal (argumentum ad populum)

   ____

   ____

   ____

   ____

2. Peruse *The **Congressional** Record*, at *http://www.access.gpo.gov/su_docs/aces/aces150.html*, and choose a speech, preferably one by your senator or representative. Read the speech and record the following:

   Speaker: ____________________ Date: ____________________

   Topic: ____________________

   Speeches to Congress are often to persuade. Describe or quote from the text to illustrate how the speaker performed any of the following methods of adapting to the audience.

   Establishing common ground ____________________

   ____

   ____

Organizing for expected response ______________________________

____

____

Adapting to hostile audience by showing understanding ______________________________

____

____

Adapting to hostile audience by the use of appropriate humor ______________________________

____

____

NAME ______________________________

HAPTER 14 SELF TEST

ATCHING I (KEY TERMS)

atch each term listed on the left with its correct definition from the column on the right.

_____ **1.** indirect persuasion
_____ **2.** character
_____ **3.** charisma
_____ **4.** common ground
_____ **5.** competence
_____ **6.** convincing
_____ **7.** credibility
_____ **8.** evidence
_____ **9.** direct persuasion
_____ **10.** emotional evidence
_____ **11.** ethical persuasion

a. persuasive strategy stressing similarities between speaker and audience
b. material used to prove a point
c. a speech goal that aims at changing audience's beliefs, values, or attitudes
d. persuasion not dependent on false or misleading information
e. persuasion which disguises or deemphasizes speaker's persuasive purpose
f. audience perception of honesty and impartiality
g. evidence that arouses strong feelings in the audience
h. a quality of credibility that stresses personal expertise and preparation
i. believability of a speaker or other information source
j. dimension of credibility that combines enthusiasm and likability
k. persuasion that does not try to hide a persuasive purpose

ATCHING II

_____ **12.** latitude of acceptance
_____ **13.** latitude of noncommitment
_____ **14.** latitude of rejection
_____ **15.** persuasion
_____ **16.** proposition of fact
_____ **17.** proposition of policy
_____ **18.** proposition of value
_____ **19.** social judgment theory
_____ **20.** strategy to actuate
_____ **21.** strategy to convince
_____ **22.** target audience

a. that part of an audience that must be influenced in order to achieve a persuasive goal
b. in social judgment theory, statements that a person would not care strongly about one way or another
c. explanation of attitude change that posits opinions will change in small increments only when the target opinions lie in the receiver's latitudes of acceptance and noncommitment
d. persuasive plan that seeks to move an audience to immediate action
e. claim in which there are two or more sides of conflicting verifiable evidence
f. persuasive strategy that seeks to change the way an audience thinks
g. in social judgment theory, statements that a person would not reject
h. in social judgment theory, statements that person would not accept
i. claim that involves adopting or rejecting a specific course of action
j. the communication act of motivating a person to change a particular belief, attitude, value, or behavior
k. claim involving the worth of an idea, a person, or an object

MULTIPLE CHOICE

Choose the BEST response from those listed.

1. Which of these is true of persuasion?

a. It is coercive.
b. It is usually incremental.
c. It is linear or one-way.
d. It is unethical.
e. all of the above

2. Following the thinking of social judgment theory, a speaker who is trying to persuade an audience will do best to appeal to propositions within the audience's

a. anchor.
b. latitude of acceptance.
c. latitude of noncommitment.
d. latitude of rejection.
e. none of the above

3. Persuasive speakers who adhere to the principles of social judgment theory tend to

a. seek realistic, if modest, goals from the audience's latitude of noncommitment.
b. seek to move audiences to accept positions now in their latitude of rejection.
c. seek to widen an audience's latitude of noncommitment.
d. all of the above
e. none of the above

4. Ethical persuasion, as defined by the text, is

a. in the best interest of the audience.
b. not dependent on false or misleading information.
c. an honest attempt to change an audience's attitude or behavior.
d. all of the above
e. none of the above

5. Which of these is unethical communication behavior as defined by the text?

a. insincerity
b. withholding information
c. plagiarism
d. relaying false information
e. all of the above

6. "Capital punishment is immoral." This is a proposition of _________.

a. fact
b. value
c. policy
d. agency
e. none of the above

7. A speech which tries to get an audience to begin buying only low-fat foods is what type?

a. convincing
b. discontinuance
c. adoption
d. all of the above
e. none of the above

8. Indirect persuasion would be most appropriate when

a. talking to a group of nonsmokers about the dangers of smoking.
b. talking to a group of Republicans about the merits of a Democratic proposal.
c. talking to students who are in class on time about the importance of promptness over tardiness.
d. talking to a group of teachers about the value of education.
e. All of the above are equally germane occasions for using indirect persuasion.

9. The purpose statement for a speech to convince will usually stress an attitude; a purpose statement for a speech to actuate will stress a/an

a. behavior.
b. evidence.
c. attitude.
d. thought.
e. Any of the above are equally appropriate for a purpose statement of a speech to actuate.

10. Assume these are three possible parts of an outline:

I. Describe the problem
II. Describe the solution
III. Describe the desired audience response

A speech to actuate would most appropriately include

a. I only.
b. I and II only.
c. I, II, and III.
d. I and III only.
e. II and III only.

11. In describing a proposed solution, which question(s) must a speaker be sure to answer?

a. What will it cost?
b. Will it work?
c. What are the advantages?
d. a and b
e. b and c

12. A **first** step in adapting to most audiences is to

a. establish common ground.
b. organize your material with your toughest area of disagreement first.
c. use humor.
d. demonstrate how your view supersedes their view.
e. use inductive reasoning.

13. Which of these represents the least biased citation?

a. The current tax rate for those with $60,000–$80,000 taxable incomes—from the current IRS tax form
b. Statistics on Chicago being one of the safest cities to live in—from a 1963 survey
c. Information to convince you of the health benefits of milk—from the Wisconsin Dairy Association
d. Your Republican senator's voting record published by the Young Republicans
e. Your Republican senator's voting record published by the Young Democrats

14. The three C's of credibility described by your text are

a. creation, completion, coordination.
b. co-existence, cooperation, completion.
c. competition, coordination, completion.
d. competence, character, and charisma.
e. collaboration, co-ordination, character.

MATCHING III (PROPOSITIONS)

Match the label of the type of proposition with the items that are examples of that type of proposition. You will use some words more than once.

fact value policy

____________ 1. The mayor did not violate campaign spending laws.

____________ 2. The United States should continue to be involved in Kosovo.

____________ 3. It is better to kill animals for research than allow humans to suffer.

____________ 4. Children's interests should come ahead of adult interests when deciding cases of dispute between biological, surrogate, or adoptive parents.

____________ 5. The United States has a higher rate of crime than any other industrialized democracy.

____________ 6. The United States should institute national health insurance.

____________ 7. There was less bloodshed in Kosovo after NATO intervention.

____________ 8. College students should get credit for volunteer work in the community.

____________ 9. College students who work at jobs up to 20 hours a week have higher grade point averages than do those who don't work at jobs at all.

____________ 10. Internships are better preparation for careers than senior seminars.

TRUE/FALSE

Circle the T or F to indicate whether you believe the statement is true or false. If it is **true**, give a **reason** or an **example**. If it is **false**, **explain** what would make it true.

T F 1. Persuasion and ethics are unrelated.

____

____

T F 2. Propositions of fact usually try to convince the audience what should be done.

____

____